Best Game Ever

MIKE GROSS

and the Lancaster Newspapers sports staff

Best Game Ever

Text by Mike Gross
and the staff of Lancaster Newspapers Inc.

Photographs by Lancaster Newspapers Inc.
Cover photo by Dan Marschka
Cover design by Chris Emlet
Printed by Intelligencer Printing Company

Published by:
Lancaster Newspapers Inc.
8 West King Street
P.O. Box 1328
Lancaster, PA 17608

ISBN Number: 978-0-615-89101-9

Index

Lancaster Newspapers Archives

Introduction

The Dec. 15, 2003, edition of the Lancaster Intelligencer Journal included a letter to the editor bemoaning the glorifying of high school football at the expense of, as the reader saw it, the anniversary of Pearl Harbor. "In another year, there will be a new state football champ," it read, "but there will never be anything to replace the memories of the attack on Pearl Harbor." Leaving aside the facts that the paper had run several pieces of Pearl Harbor remembrance the previous week, that this particular reader has been a regular and enthusiastic bemoaner of things, and that his recollection of Pearl Harbor ("there will never be anything to replace the memories") seems disturbingly wistful — the reader has a point, one noted by no less than William Faulkner in a 1955 Sports Illustrated essay on the Kentucky Derby. Of that Derby day, he wrote, "So it is not the Day after all. It is only the 81st one."

It is axiomatic, in modern

Jeremy Smith and a teammate celebrate in the snow.

America, far more than in Faulkner's, that there is too much sport. Too many teams, leagues, games and playoff berths. Too many seasons, pre-, post- and regular. Too many team camps and showcases and combines and drafts and trade deadlines. Overkill was left for dead decades ago. To put a finer point on it, there are 43 state high school team championships to be won in Pennsylvania annually. Almost annually, a local school wins at least one of them. If you missed that championship, sit tight. Another one is coming, ad infinitum. So why a book about this one? There are a number of small reasons.

Manheim Central's state title was then Lancaster County's only state high school football title, and football is the marquee high school sport, certainly in Pennsylvania. There are some remarkable people in this story, and what's remarkable about them has been forged or developed or put on display by their commitment to a team and a game. This is in no way "Friday Night Lights" revisited, but it is a story about how a game can be woven so tightly into a town's fabric that grappling hooks couldn't pull it free. There are, inevitably, elements of race and culture and sociology. Manheim Central's season, its run to the state championship game, was remarkable enough on its own, especially in the context of the program's rich, colorful history.

Those are the small reasons. The big one is the actual game: the 2003 Class AAA state football championship between Manheim Central and Pine-Richland. It's the best game I've ever seen. It's the best game most people who saw it have ever seen. Not the best high school game, not the best football game, but the *best game*. I am tempted here to argue that point, to canvass sports history and drive home the case, but because this book is not an argument or even one side of one, I will give in to that urge only to say this: In the company of all the very best games ever played, Manheim Central/Pine-Richland has in common all the good stuff — spectacle, drama, suspense and what can only, if inadequately, be called brilliance. Its conclusion brought elation and disappointment, utter satisfaction and the aching absence of it, as acutely as they can be felt. It is distinct, in this company, because it was played by teenage kids in a blizzard.

It is not nearly the most famous high-stakes football game played in the worst of winter. But the more famous ones, the ones played by adult professionals, are known less for the football than the weather itself, its limiting impact or eccentric fallout. Think of the frozen tundra of Lambeau Field (neither frozen nor, by definition, tundra), the Tuck Rule (wasn't a tuck, shouldn't have been a rule) and that game-winning field goal in New England in 1982, which, in addition to occurring in the mere regular season, comes with a snowplow-shaped asterisk. Manheim Central/Pine-Richland soared above the weather, even as it was elegantly framed by it. They played and played, and the snow fell and wind howled, and there was something crazy and unprecedented and even mystical about how it looked and felt. Robert Lombardi, the current executive director of the Pennsylvania Interscholastic Athletic Association, was hardly the first to observe that, "It was like watching a game in a snow globe."

"I think what amazed people was that they thought nobody would be able to do anything," Manheim Central coach Mike Williams said, looking back 10 years later. "As it turned out, everybody did everything." About 5,000 people saw it in person, but many more, thanks to Pennsylvania Cable Network, saw it live or in replay on television. It resonated, and reached far beyond the usual prep-football crowd. I attended two holiday gatherings that year, nowhere near Manheim with not a single Baron or high school football fan in the house, parties at which not a single other sports-related topic was discussed for one second. In both cases, with no prompting from or toward me and for no evident reason, someone brought up Manheim Central/Pine-Richland. In both cases, the reaction was the same: shrieks. "Oh, my God … Did you see that game?" Pearl Harbor never came up, although one senses it's been adequately chronicled.

Yes, there is too much sport. But of this kind, there will never be enough.

Mike Gross
June 2013

Mike Williams gets ready to turn the Barons loose on each other at practice.

Chapter 1:
The Jersey

There's no question when and where this story culminates: in Hershey, Pa., in a blizzard on Dec. 5, 2003. Where it begins is debatable. Perhaps in August of that year, where every football story can begin, in training camp. Perhaps it goes back to 1981, when Mike Williams became Central's head football coach. Or even back to the early 1960s, when Williams, as a child growing up in Manheim, realized he wanted to be a coach someday. He had always been the guy in the neighborhood organizing other kids for sports, and by junior high school, he knew what he wanted to do.

For reasons that will soon enough be obvious, let's begin in the summer of 1997, with a charismatic 11-year-old from Manheim named Shawn Wilt. "Charismatic" is Williams' word. "Shawn has always been the kid who, when he walks into a room, the room lights up," Williams said. Wilt wasn't a great athlete then,

now or in 2003. He did not have exceptional speed or strength. He didn't
start at Central until his senior year. But he did love football, its frenzied
action, the ferocity of it, the camaraderie that came with playing it with your
friends. Over time, Wilt's intelligence and will and passion and taste for action evolved, and he became a superb two-way player with graduate-level
football instincts and a sense of the moment. Ironically, he played the posi-
tions of wide receiver and defensive back, where pure athleticism counts
most. "He was one of those kids coaches are al-
ways looking for, who don't necessarily have the
most talent," Williams said. "But, put him on the
field, in a game ..."

"Shawn (Wilt) has always
been the kid who, when
he walks into a room, the
room lights up."

Mike Williams

In 1997, Wilt was just a sixth-grader, attend-
ing the Junior Baron Football Camp. There was a
Camper of the Week award given by the coaches,
and Wilt won it. The prize was a jersey, game-
worn in the Hula Bowl and autographed by Mike Ruhl, a massive lineman
who had played at Manheim Central and the University of Tulsa. "It had
grass stains on it and everything," Wilt said. "Very cool." When camp was
over, Wilt and his mom were walking back to the car, Wilt carrying his
jersey. Williams walked by and chatted a bit. He jokingly offered to buy the

The Barons charge on to the field to battle Lower Dauphin for the District 3 championship.

jersey from Wilt for $50. Wilt says now he can't believe what came out of his 11-year-old mouth. "No way I'm selling it, Coach," he said. "When we win the state championship, when I'm a senior, I'll give it to you."

Not if. When.

Manheim Central was an established power by 1997, but it had never even played for a state championship. Wilt took the jersey home and put it in his closet. It stayed there, on a hanger, for six years. In December 2003, at Manheim Central's postseason football banquet, Wilt asked for speaking time. He walked to the dais carrying a box. He told the story of the camp, then opened the box. "Coach," he said, "I'm a man of my word."

Shawn Wilt and his mother, Sharon

Chapter 2:

Manheim

The first symbol of Baron football in Manheim as you drive into town from the north on Route 72 comes even before the standard Chamber of Commerce sign welcoming visitors. "Home of the Barons, 2003 State Champs" is painted on the side of The Hubcap Barn. Drive another couple blocks into downtown proper, as Route 72 narrows and becomes Main Street, and in autumn you pass Baron football posters affixed to lampposts and telephone poles. They're the work of the MOB, Mothers of Barons, who create banners honoring Central's players, coaches, managers and cheerleaders.

Another acronym of note is MTC, for Manheim Touchdown Club, a group of local football boosters formed in 1998 "for the purpose of development, promotion and support of Manheim scholastic football, including recognition and financial aid for exceptional student athletes within the greater community," according to its website. MTC funded a $60,000 scoreboard, complete with an electronic message board, for Manheim Central's Elden Rettew Field in 1999. It has continued to fund capital projects for the football program, weight room improvements and the like, but has since grown and branched out to provide scholarships — not all to football players, or even necessarily to MC kids. Guest speakers at its annual awards banquet have included Nick Saban and Gene Upshaw.

This is not to portray unhealthy preoccupation. Manheim loves the Barons, but there's little evidence of obsession. It's a small town, in the Rust Belt but also in Pennsylvania Dutch country, neither blighted nor retrofitted for hipsters nor self-consciously charming. People have lives. Off the main drag, there are ranch homes and split-levels along tree-lined streets. Nearby are cornfields and grazing cows. Narrow row houses and small businesses line Main Street: Nearly-Nu Thrift Shop, Style Mosaic, Hope Fire Company (perhaps raffling a pickup truck), JoBoy's Brew Pub, Pretentious Hairstyles.

Wait … yes, *Pretentious* Hairstyles.

Manheim's history predates the American Revolution. It was originally laid out in 1762 by Henry William Stiegel, a glassmaker and ironmaster of some renown. Stiegel had business failures (which didn't stop him from dubbing himself a "baron," thus giving the school district its eventual mascot), and the town didn't take off until the Reading and Columbia Railroad came through in the Civil War era. The population has hovered around 5,000 — mostly white, mostly working class — for decades.

Manheim is about 10 miles south of Lebanon and the same distance north of Lancaster. Harrisburg is about 35 miles northwest, Reading is roughly the same distance to the north and York is 25 miles west. In all of those places are high schools that were once part of the Central Penn League, an all-sports conference of high schools in medium-size Pennsylvania industrial towns that, according to the late Joe Paterno, erstwhile patriarch of football in the state, "played the best high school football in the country." The league was part of a rich tradition of the sport in Pennsylvania, generating names like Namath, Ditka, Bednarik, Unitas and Montana.

Manheim Central? Not so much. District and state football playoffs didn't exist until the 1980s in Pennsylvania, and the school competed in the Conference of the Roses, which was a big deal locally but not beyond. Central had a solid athletic tradition through most of the 20th century, but it was more known for wrestling than football before Williams returned to town to coach and teach in the 1980s. The Central Penn League peaked in the middle of the century, as the steel industry thrived and attracted tough, blue-collar ethnic families that valued sports, especially football. (Steelton, the smallest and perhaps grittiest CPL town, was literally built around a Bethlehem Steel plant near Harrisburg along the Susquehanna River.) John Harris High School in Harrisburg became a national power in the 1960s, sending an All-American quarterback, Jimmy Jones, to USC, and an all-American receiver, Jan White, to Ohio State. Coach George Chaump followed White to Columbus, as an assistant coach to Woody Hayes. Chaump is considered the main voice in talking Hayes into modernizing his

> *"Home of the Barons, 2003 State Champs"*
>
> … painted on the side of The Hubcap Barn

thinking and throwing the ball once in a while with quarterback Rex Kern — a strategy that led to the Buckeyes' 1968 national championship.

By the 1970s, the steel industry was dying, its plants and the towns surrounding them rusting over. The Lancaster-Lebanon League formed in 1972 and included CPL dropouts Lancaster McCaskey and Lebanon. By 1978, the Central Penn was defunct. Into the big-school power vacuum in Pennsylvania football came suburban mergers (Cumberland Valley, Central Bucks West, Penn Hills, etc.) and private schools (Erie Cathedral Prep, Bishop McDevitt and assorted Central Catholics). District Three playoffs came in 1982. The Pennsylvania Interscholastic Athletic Association added a fourth enrollment class, AAAA, in 1985. The sprawling Western Pennsylvania Interscholastic Athletic League and the other 10 PIAA districts made a workable framework for state playoffs, which began in 1988. With four classes, there was still plenty of room for small-town schools to thrive. Southern Columbia High, in tiny Catawissa, has won six Class A state titles, including five in a row from 2002 to 2006. Mount Carmel, the longtime Coal Region power, won state AA championships every other year from 1994 through 2002. Of course, there were Berwick (six state titles and three USA Today national titles) and Strath Haven (four straight state finals and two championships from 1999 to 2002) in AAA.

A poster by MOB, or Mothers of Barons

All of this evolved at a good time for Manheim Central's program, which Williams was building into a monster in the 1980s. Manheim did not get hammered as hard as other towns by the decline of industrial manufacturing, partly because of its surrounding agriculture. Manheim Central School District did not have the tax-base problems of many rural school districts, partly because of the proximity of bigger towns, but also because of the Manheim Auto Auction, which by 2000 was the world's largest by sales volume. The auction was Manheim's largest employer,

Watching from afar at Lyndon Diner in Manheim are, from left, Jacqueline Lowery, Tammy Anderson and Monica Anderson.

and the economic engine that drew smaller businesses. The auction turned Manheim, economically, into a car town. Along Route 72 between Hubcap Barn on the north end of town to the auction on the south end, a stretch of less than three miles, there are 27 car dealers or auto-related businesses, not counting gas stations.

It makes for an interesting mix: tough farm and blue-collar kids willing to hit the weight room and opponents, and families with the right combination of work ethic and enough room in their lives to prioritize a sport.

"Compare Manheim to Lititz," said Williams, referring to the borough's neighbor to the east, which was named America's Coolest Small Town in 2013 by Budget Travel magazine. "They have beautiful homes, lots of professional people.

"We have nice homes, too, of course, but we have a lot of blue-collar pride. What makes Manheim different is the work ethic installed by the parents in the kids. We hold our kids accountable, ask them to do a lot. They still seem to be willing to do it. We hear all the time from other coaches how hard a time they have getting kids to do this or that. We kind of smile inside. We have issues. Not every kid wants to do everything. But not too many people outwork us.

You may work as hard, but nobody outworks us."

Going into the 2003 season, Central had won 12 District Three Class AAA championships in 14 years. It had been blocked, at the semifinal level of the state playoffs, by Berwick and Strath Haven. In other words, it was blocked, within its rough demographic of medium-to-large, nonurban public schools, by two of the best in the country.

Pine-Richland is in a white-collar suburb of Pittsburgh. The contrast with Manheim is acute. "It's a very rich neighborhood, kind of aristocratic," Clair Altemus, P-R's coach in 2003, said. "The facilities we had were tremendous. Anything we wanted. They believe money can buy you anything, and they want to stand at the watercooler and say they kicked somebody's ass Friday night."

Another difference: Before 2003, Pine-Richland hadn't won so much as an outright league championship in 30 years.

Mike Williams in 2013

Chapter 3:
The Prayer

Football coaches are decision-makers. Williams had made thousands of them by December 2003, when he arrived back at a place he had been too often: a tight, tense battle against a Goliath of an opponent for a berth in a state championship game. He was in the visitors' locker room at Coatesville High School. Outside, the afternoon was viciously cold and windy, with gusts to 45 miles per hour. The night before, rain had bombarded the field, which was hopelessly muddy, barely playable. The conditions forced a weirdly miniaturized version of football: Inches were like yards, first downs were like points and field position was the holy grail. It was halftime, and Central led 3-0.

In this round of the state football playoffs, the semifinals, Central was 0-8. In the back of Williams' mind — perhaps it was always back there — was Central's history in those games, and within that history Williams' track record as a maker of hard, high-stakes choices. It's hard to think of any fabulously successful football coach at any level whose legacy contains so many high-stakes, highly debated choices. In the 1994 Eastern Pennsylvania final (a state semifinal game), Central lost 37-30 to Berwick, then the top AAA programs in the sport in Pennsylvania. It was a classic. The level of football over four quarters was as good as any state playoff game played to that point. But Central faced a first-

and-goal from the Berwick 4-yard line with 38 seconds left. Williams called one of his two remaining timeouts. He had a future NFL fullback, Dan Kreider, in his backfield along with Craig Dougherty, another excellent runner. But the Barons had outgained and largely outplayed Berwick, in part, by surprising the Bulldogs with a run-and-shoot passing game. "The kids wanted to run the ball," Williams said. "But we only had one timeout left, and I wanted to save that. If we get stopped, then you've got to use your timeout." Williams opted for a pass, which was intercepted in the end zone. Berwick went on to win the state title, beating Sharon in the final, 27-7. A year later, again in the Eastern final, again against Berwick, Central led 17-6 with 1:25 left in the third quarter and faced a fourth-and-goal at the Berwick 3-yard line. A field goal — an extra-point-length kick — would have given Central a two-touchdown lead. Williams went for the touchdown. The Barons got stuffed and ended up losing, 18-17. Again, Berwick won it all the following week, again routing Sharon, 43-6.

It isn't so much that everyone else questions Williams in these moments; it's that he openly, publicly, endearingly questions himself. "I second-guess myself a lot in close games," he admitted. After the 37-30 loss to Berwick in '94, he said, "I guess it was a lousy call if you look back on it. Maybe we should have run it. Maybe Kreider would have rolled into the end zone, or Dougherty. I don't know."

Strath Haven beat Central 30-21 in 1999, in yet another state semifinal, and the Panthers went on to, yes, win the state championship. It had been 21-21 late in the third quarter, Central driving and running the ball effectively, when Williams dialed up a pass. There was an interception, and then an unraveling, and then Williams standing before the media again, explaining. "It's hard to talk right now," he said, red-eyed. "It's as disappointing as it can possibly be." And then: "Maybe we should have kept it on the ground."

There was a 96-0 defeat of Solanco that year, and the routine assumption that, given that score, Williams had to have been running up the score, bullying a hapless opponent. He had his judgment questioned by everyone from his own school's principal to an editorialist for the Lancaster McCaskey High School Vidette. "That was probably the biggest regret of my career," he said.

Even what amounts to a lifetime achievement award for Pennsylvania coaches — coaching the home side in the Big 33 all-star game against Ohio — ended with mixed emotions when Williams was at the helm in 1996. Pennsylvania gave up 38 points in the first half to Ohio, and there was grumbling in the home bleachers throughout a 45-36 loss. "This is not our team," Williams said afterward. "But I know people out there probably said I'm pretty stupid and all kinds of things. I had a good experience. But like any coach who does this game, you're quite happy when the week's over and you can go back to your own players."

All of that is small stuff compared to 2001, another state semifinal, this time against Strath Haven, which had replaced Berwick as the state AAA benchmark. The Panthers utterly dominated the first half, pushing Central around at will. They led at halftime, 14-0 — and it could've been worse. But the Barons found something at the break. Incredibly, they didn't allow a first down after halftime. They scored with 56 seconds left to pull within 14-13. Williams decided to go for a two-point conversion and win it outright, in regulation, rather than tie the game and go to overtime. The two-point pass attempt failed. Strath Haven won and, naturally, went on to win the state championship.

As coaches go, Williams is not superstitious. He does not, at least superficially, tend toward the spiritual. He is something of a sports scientist: He believes in data, knowing the latest research and methods, and constantly adapting. But before the 2001 Strath Haven game, on the field at Coatesville High, Williams found a religious medal with an image of the Virgin Mary inscribed on it. The medallion was somehow shiny and clean. He put it in his pocket. "I figured that had to be a good omen," he said. "Turned out it wasn't." At halftime, Williams and his staff were as stunned as they were disappointed, to have watched their players be not just dominated, but physically beaten up. They barely said a word to them. Then the officials stopped by to tell the Barons they had to be on the field in a minute, and the scientist in Williams was trumped by the romantic.

Williams told the players how disappointed he was. He reminded the seniors that this could be the last football game they'll ever play. He challenged their toughness, their commitment, their understanding of what they represented. He didn't show them the medal, but he never stopped thinking about it. Swept up, he told them that if they somehow turned the game around, if they found a way to score twice, if they had the chance at the end of the game, they'd go for two and win it right then and there. When in fact Central did all that, well … "I thought about halftime, the medal, what seemed like a prophecy," Williams said, remembering and chuckling at how that sounds 12 years later. "You're in the locker room, doing what you can with kids to try to get them back in the game. The 'We'll go for two' was almost like an afterthought. But then … that's what happened. In the immature mind of a coach, sometimes you believe in fate." And sometimes fate stomps on your belief like it's an empty beer can.

On the ride home, the bus passed over a creek. Williams thought for a crazy moment of having the driver stop, so he could throw the Virgin Mary in the water. He didn't, and it's been in his office ever since. "It was one of the worst weekends of my life," he said. There was only one letter to the newspaper, ripping Williams, in the aftermath. He received no angry calls, even though his home number was in the book. He did receive consoling calls from former players. When he walked into a booster club meeting the following week, he received a sustained ovation. He was putting up Christmas lights at his house when the mother of a player approached, but not to rip him. "She said she just wanted to give me a hug," he said. Still, Williams hammered himself. "If two guys say you're a terrible coach, you personally magnify that," he said. "A decision that was made — mine, I felt like — cost our school the victory. I took it very personally."

A small irony here is that game theory, backed by research, suggests the odds favor football coaches going for two points far more often than they actually do. A huge irony is that two nearly identical decisions by Williams 12 years before had dramatically worked and propelled Manheim Central into the big time. On the last day of the 1989 regular season, Central and Elizabethtown met at E-town, both sides undefeated, the Section Two title on the line. It was a back-and-forth affair, but Central scored in the fourth quarter to pull within 14-13. Williams went for two. Quarterback Chad Ginder cashed it in on an option run. The Barons won, 15-14. The same teams met two weeks later in Hershey for the district championship. Central trailed 14-7 in that game, late in the fourth quarter, on third-and-8 from the E-town 39. A Ginder pass was intercepted. Central's Neil Fittery, a superb two-way player, hit the interceptor and knocked the ball

As a high-stakes decision-maker, Mike Williams, left, and opposite, often questioned himself.

loose. Ginder recovered and ran 28 yards for a touchdown with 2:49 left. Williams went for two again. Again it worked. Again the Barons won, 15-14. It put Central in the state playoffs, opposite nationally ranked Berwick. The Barons, utterly unknown at the state level then, baffled Berwick for a half, led 10-0, and pushed the Bulldogs to the limit before losing, 14-10. "That was the most pivotal point in our whole history of football here at Manheim," Williams said. "It put our program on the map. I guess Mike Williams was a genius then."

Fourteen years later in Coatesville, he didn't feel like one, in the wind and cold, at halftime, clinging to that 3-0 lead. The refs stopped by the locker room to ask Williams whether he wanted the wind at his back in the third quarter or the fourth. There's no science to that particular choice: It's 50/50. Except that on this day, the wind was as big a factor in a football game as Dick Butkus or Red Grange or Vince Lombardi had ever been. Williams chose to give Strath Haven the wind in the third quarter, so he could have it in the fourth. Then players, coaches and officials trudged back into the cold. Williams stayed by himself in the quiet for a long moment. "I said a little prayer," he said. "Whether you call it superstitious or spiritual, it was difficult, based on past ex-perience. I don't know ... just, 'Dear Lord, help me make the right call.' "

Or, more precisely, *help the call I just made be right.*

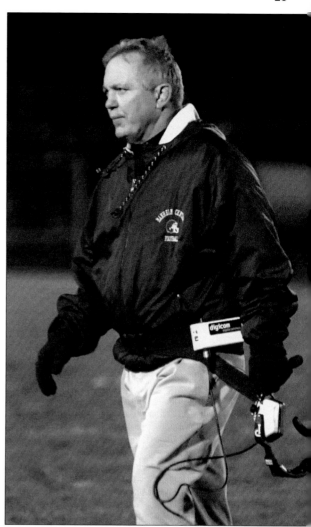

Chapter 4:
Creating a Monster

By 2003, high school football had long since become a 12-month-a-year project. Many football coaches, especially ones who've been around for a while, grudgingly tolerate the offseason grind, or farm it out to younger assistants. Williams loves it. "We do try to keep up to date," he said. "We're always trying to learn. I like the scientific stuff of trying to make a kid a better athlete. Some coaches just want to coach the quarterbacks, or the defense, or the linemen. I want to do it all." His teams tried to do it all. Whereas most prep powers are known for either running straight at defenses or around them, or throwing the ball over them, Manheim Central does some of everything: the veer-option, the spread and even some elements of the doughty old Wing T.

Central rarely had more size or speed than opponents at the highest level. It compensated with execution, and by being hard to prepare for. It not only tried to do more than everyone else, it tried to do it better. "We never think we're blessed with the best athletes in America," Williams

> *"We're always trying to learn. I like the scientific stuff of trying to make a kid a better athlete. Some coaches just want to coach the quarterbacks, or the defense, or the linemen. I want to do it all."*
>
> Mike Williams

Central quarterback
Jarryd Moyer

Offense didn't figure to be an issue for the '03 Barons.

said. "We try to find any advantage we can. I like that part of it." The formula derailed, just a little, in 2002. The 2001 team had been one of Williams' best. It lost by a point to Strath Haven (recall the decision, down 14-13, to go for two) in the state semis and featured one of Central's best defenses, a unit that held the nationally ranked Panthers without a first down in the second half.

In 2002, defense was an issue. The Barons were fine at quarterback, with Jarryd Moyer throwing for nearly 1,700 yards, running for 744 and accounting for 31 touchdowns. It had runners (Corby Ziegler) and receivers (Rich Shellenberger, Danny Thythavong) and the core of a superb line in Mike Byrne, Kevin Hershey, Rob Trovato and Kevin Krause. Central opened the season at Central Dauphin, a suburban Harrisburg Class AAAA school that has since emerged as, arguably, the top all-sports power in Pennsylvania. Central Dauphin would win the District Three AAAA title that year, and it blasted the Barons on opening night, 51-22. Central entered the league portion of its schedule 1-2, having lost to local rival Hempfield, 26-10, in Week 3.

The Barons rolled through Section Two, the only serious test a 30-20 home win over archrival Conestoga Valley in Week 9. Despite Central's flaws, it seemed to be on a familiar path as the postseason began, against Lower Dauphin at Hersheypark Stadium. The Barons led that game 17-0. They led 24-13 at halftime, and 40-36 with 75 seconds left. But the defense couldn't stop Lower Dauphin from making big plays. The last of them, a Matt Ruffner-to-Chris Albright pass in the end zone as time expired, beat Central, 43-40. After 10 straight district titles, Central had been beaten on the first night of the postseason. It finished a pedestrian 8-3. That moment, as Lower Dauphin celebrated, was when the '03 season symbolically began. "It killed us," said Krause, then a junior offensive lineman, and today Central's head JV coach. "Ten straight district titles ... There was a lot of pressure, a lot of responsibility on our shoulders. It was tough to take, the feeling that we let people down. As a junior class, we thought those seniors were great, and we weren't able to do enough."

The '03 team included 18 seniors. They were not, on the face of it, a group that stood out by Central standards. The class had some big kids, like Byrne and the farm-boy twins, Kevin and Neil Hershey. But those three didn't play youth league football some years as they moved through the ranks because they were too big, exceeding weight restrictions. Jarryd Moyer started playing quar-
terback in the Manheim leagues at age 10, but he rarely played behind the big guys, most of whom played junior high football in eighth grade. When Moyer was a freshman, the junior high team went just 4-4. As a senior, Moyer was a big quarterback (6-4, 205) who could run and throw, but he threw 11 interceptions his junior year. As the 2003 season approached, no one compared him to the greatest Central QBs, like Jeff Smoker, a national recruit who was at Michigan State at the time, or Matt Nagy, who played at Delaware and in the Arena League and is today the Kansas City Chiefs' quarterbacks coach. Most of the key skill-position players had graduated. Glaringly missing was perhaps the quintessential Central player, the fullback/linebacker type who set a physical tone on and off the field.

Jarryd Moyer emerged as a passer, runner and leader in '03.

The archetype was Dan Kreider, who played eight years in the NFL and got a Super Bowl ring as the Pittsburgh Steelers' starting fullback in 2008.

There were things to like. Nine starters were back on defense. Byrne (6-5, 265), the Hersheys (each around 6-4, 235), tackle Rob Trovato (6-1, 275) and Krause (5-10, 210) were the nucleus of a big, tough offensive front that bonded with their coach, Dave Hahn, and committed to pushing each other on the field and in the weight room. The Barons had a lot of things going for them, but the offensive line is the engine of a football team, and it emerged as Central's best position-group before the season even started. "We definitely had chemistry," Neil Hershey said. "It was a driven group. We all made every one of our lifting sessions that summer." In preseason camp in August, Williams generally puts his teams through three sessions a day. The first two were two hours long, the last an hour. Several times that summer, he gave the offensive-line regulars the middle session off. "I think he felt we had earned that. We had a chance to be a special group, and we had earned his respect," Hershey said.

At some point in June 2003, Williams met with Brian Hunter, a man from York whose sons, Jeremiha and Xzavier, were football players. The older, Jer-

emiha, already had a reputation based on his freshman season at York's William Penn High. Brian Hunter had been a star player at York, and had coached at the youth league level. He said he decided to move his family after his young daughter had been jumped from behind and beaten in York. The Hunters decided to move to Manheim, where he said they owned land. The boys would attend Central and play for the Barons. Williams made Brian Hunter a volunteer assistant coach. Jeremiha was 6-2, 190, and it soon became clear he was the fastest kid on the team. Williams had often, in the

Sophomore Jeremiha Hunter

past, bemoaned the absence on his roster of the one player who could change the game with sheer athleticism. Now, maybe, he had that player. Maybe he'd get hammered for it — it certainly looked from the outside like one of those "athletic transfers" people roll their eyes over, especially the part about making Dad an assistant coach — but maybe Jeremiha Hunter could give the Barons a dimension they never had before.

Williams said the Manheim Central administration was fanatical about handling the transfer by the book. When the house the Hunters were having built in Manheim wasn't finished, for example, the school insisted the family rent an apartment in Manheim, to adhere to PIAA change-of-residence rules. "Everything by the book," Williams said. "They took no chance on doing anything illegal." Meanwhile, the senior football players went to work making Jeremiha part of the family. "There were about a half a dozen of us," Byrne said. "We took it upon ourselves to keep him around us all summer. We'd go get him at his house, and he'd hang out with us all day long. He was a super-nice kid, soft-spoken, but he was actually pretty funny. And it was obvious almost right away that he was a fantastic young talent."

Interior line anchor Mike Byrne

More big guys up front: Neil, left, and twin brother Kevin Hershey

Despite all that, the biggest reasons for optimism as the season approached were intangible. "The camaraderie was unbelievable," Wilt said. "We were all close, all friends. There weren't too many conflicts. We really worked at making sure the younger guys hung with us. We had our all-stars, but other Central teams had more talent. We were well-rounded, really a team. Especially now, having been around a little bit, I realize there was something special about it."

There were honor students all over the roster, and Byrne and the Hersheys, in particular, devoured the strongest advanced-placement classes Manheim Central had to offer. "I was by far the stupidest guy on the offensive line," said a self-deprecating Trovato. "I think our team's intelligence was more outstanding that our size or strength." Defensive coordinator John Brubaker recalled not having to rerun a lot of plays or revisit drills. "They understood what it took, understood that their time was limited, that if you had a bad practice, you can't get it back."

They never needed to get it back, it turned out. "That team never had a single bad practice," Williams said. "Some days were better than others, of course, but every day, we walked off the field feeling like we got done what we wanted to. I've never seen that, before or since."

"We talked about it as a staff that summer. We decided, and Mike made the conscious effort to say, 'Hey, let's shoot for the moon here. Let's put it out there. Let's put a big goal out there.'"

John Brubaker
Defensive coordinator

Considering the unique attitudes and abilities of this team, Williams approached the 2003 season differently. Before, he had been self-consciously quiet about goals. In talking to the players and the media, he avoided even using the words "state championship." No longer. "We talked about it as a staff that summer," Brubaker said. "We decided, and Mike made the conscious effort to say, 'Hey, let's shoot for the moon here. Let's put it out there. Let's put a big goal out there.' " Williams saw it as a natural approach: He had intelligent kids, good workers and a mature team, so why not build the idea that this was a special group?

Byrne and a few other seniors had been part of the 2001 team. Almost all of the Barons had been around the program for years. They knew how good, and how committed, previous editions had been. "We didn't knew how good you had to be to win it all," Byrne said, "but I know that '01 team was really good. I know I felt like, geez, if they couldn't win it. ... Before, (Williams) never talked about that stuff. Now he talked about it all the time. I think he was trying to give us confidence, and it worked."

Not everybody needed it. "We had such a good bond," Moyer said. "I thought we were more of a team than any of the others, and we had that great offensive line. I wasn't worried about (winning) districts or the league. I knew we would do that. What I cared about was states."

"He was a quarterback," Trovato said. "He had to think like that."

Ryan Dennes, above, and Eric Meyers, below, help the Barons roll past Central Dauphin.

Chapter 5:
The Regular Season

The two losses from 2002 that stung most were both to teams from the sprawling Mid-Penn Conference: the season opener to Central Dauphin and the season ender, in districts, to Lower Dauphin. In 2003, Central Dauphin had only three starters back, and the game was at Manheim this time. The Barons, aching to hit somebody other than themselves, and still cognizant of the previous season, were beyond ready. Central got the ball first and went 83 yards in six plays — including a 51-yard run by Jarryd Moyer on a play from Page 1 of the veer-option playbook — for a touchdown. The tone for the game, and the regular season, was set. It wasn't a seamless performance. Central had eight penalties and didn't score in the second half until it recovered an onside kick in the waning minutes. It didn't rack up huge offensive numbers. Tyler McCauley had three touchdowns but only 32 rushing yards. Central Dauphin actually had more first downs. But Williams came out of that 30-3 win knowing two things: He had an offensive line, and it looked like he was going to have a defense. Jeremiha Hunter hardly touched the ball on offense. At linebacker, he forced one fumble with a savage hit, and broke up a lateral pass for another turnover.

The following week Central was better, in a 35-0 romp at Middletown. The Barons outgained the Blue Raiders 423-114, had 20 first downs and only one turnover. They led 32-0 early in the third quarter. In sports writer Ed Gruver's story in the Intelligencer Journal, Middletown coach Mike Donghia said Central was much stronger than last year. "We should be," Williams responded. "We have some guys who are pretty studly up front."

Next up: Hempfield at Manheim, a neighboring rival that had announced it was dropping Central in 2004 in order to add a Class AAAA nonleague opponent to gain district-playoff ranking points. Williams didn't like how it was handled. "We should have had a little more discussion as to how it came about," Williams said. "Anybody can drop us; it's just a question of how you do it." The move gave Williams something he dearly loves, a source of extra motivation. He says he didn't dwell on it with the kids "because it was more of an adult thing." He and Hempfield coach Tom Getz were and are friendly enough that Getz is on Williams' staff today as a volunteer assistant. But Williams did point out in the pregame locker room that the Black Knights had beaten them the year before and that Central might not get another shot at them for a long time. The result: Central 55, Hempfield 6. The Barons had a hair under 500 yards of offense and threw the ball just six times.

The nonleague portion of the schedule was over, and Central had outscored three solid opponents 120-9. "Those were some decent teams in our nonleague games," Byrne said. "We knew we had taken care of business." Williams hadn't even gone deep into the playbook. He was using a squadron of skill-position players, none of whom had impressive individual stats, but 10 of whom had already scored touchdowns. The Barons were physically beating people up and were as overwhelming a favorite to roll through Lancaster-Lebanon League Section Two as they had ever been.

The linemen on both sides of the ball, but especially the O-line, were driving the bus and becoming a tight fraternity. Before every home game, the offensive linemen would hit A&M

Eric Meyers in flight

Pizza, an Italian eatery on the town square with world-class sandwiches, grab a bunch of food and take it to Coach Hahn's house. "We wouldn't even talk about football," Trovato said. "We'd just sit there and eat and watch ESPN Classic. If we were brothers, (Hahn) was our dad."

The first four section games, against Lebanon, Warwick, Elizabethtown and Garden Spot, followed an increasingly familiar script: four straight blowouts in which the Barons yielded a combined 16 points. There were bumps and bruises. Krause sprained a knee. Tight end Kevin Yeagle missed a couple games with an appendectomy. Coach emeritus Paul "Scooter" Graham — not actually a coach, but a retired Central teacher who is still an unofficial part of the program — had to be taken from the Garden Spot game in an ambulance after breaking a leg in a sideline collision. But overall, it had been easy. That was about to change.

Ephrata has rarely been a tough opponent over the four decades of Lancaster-Lebanon League football. But in 2003, the Mounts went to Manheim on a rainy night in October ready for a fight. Ephrata was 3-1 in the section, 5-2 overall. The team featured running back Nate Rock, a passing game built around QB Derek Dubbs and wideout Ryan Bramble, and a strong defense. Maybe Central was looking ahead to a trip to once-beaten archrival Conestoga Valley the following week, but Ephrata turned out to be the one game, before the state playoffs, that the Barons actually could have lost. Central scored first, and Ephrata matched it. The Mounts went for two and missed, forcing themselves, critically, to go for two (and fail) on all subsequent TDs. Central outrushed Ephrata 341-57.

The Mounts had five critical turnovers in the rain and mud, but they got an 82-yard kickoff return, an 82-yard run from Rock and a 70-yard Dubbs-to-Bramble connection.

It was 22-18, the difference all point-after attempts, late in the third quarter. In the final seconds of the period, Central got a superb pooch punt from Jeremy Smith and then stuffed Rock, pushing him into his own end zone for a safety, a call vehemently disputed by Ephrata coach Ken Grove. There were six turnovers in the fourth quarter, as conditions worsened. The one that mattered most was a Hunter interception, returned 37 yards for a clinching touchdown. Hunter was emerging on both sides of the ball. He ran for 141 yards, and the touchdown was his ninth in five section games. The Barons got by, 28-18. It felt like a potential tipping point in the season, not in a good way, and not only because the score bespoke Central's potential vulnerability.

Shawn Wilt went down in the second quarter after attempting to tackle Bramble, and stayed there in agony for what seemed like a half-hour. Finally, his leg was placed in an inflatable cast, and Wilt was taken by ambulance to the hospital. "I was about to make a tackle, and I could see (Craig) Gatchell coming over to make it," Wilt said, recalling the play. "I eased up. Gatchell's helmet hit my knee. My fault." A broken femur was the rumored diagnosis, perhaps because that's supposedly the most painful break a human can suffer. Maybe a torn knee ligament as well. Wilt had been one of Moyer's many reliable targets as a wide receiver, and a fiery playmaker at safety. He was second on the team with 62 tackles, first with four interceptions, and he called the defensive coverages. At the hospital, Wilt's injury was diagnosed as a broken fibula, which was not good, but not as bad as a broken femur. The reason for the incredible pain was that Wilt's meniscus had slipped and was lodged against his knee joint. A doctor popped the meniscus back into place, and Wilt's pain went from, say, 33 on a scale of 10 to perhaps 8 or 9. Media accounts had Wilt likely finished for the year. Naturally, he started thinking about playing again. As Central hit the weight room Saturday to prepare for a showdown with Conestoga Valley, Wilt tore into six-days-a-week rehab.

Conestoga Valley was Central's chief rival in Section Two. CV was the only L-L school to play for a state title, when it lost 29-20 to Erie Strong Vincent in the 1991 AAA final. Their games were always among the most anticipated of the L-L season, especially when Jim Cantafio, a colorful passing-game guru, coached the Buckskins. Cantafio was out of the picture by 2003, but CV had an athletic quarterback, Jordan Steffy, who would play at the University of Maryland. An upset loss to Lebanon was the only blemish on CV's resume. While Central was struggling with Ephrata, Steffy was throwing six touchdown passes in a 46-0 destruction of Elizabethtown.

CV's stadium was packed to the rafters for the showdown, moved to a windy, gloomy Saturday night to facilitate a local television broadcast. For the

Increasingly, as the year wore on, Mike Williams turned Jeremiha Hunter loose.

first time, Central faced a team that could match it on the line of scrimmage. CV had more first downs and held Central to a modest 208 yards. Steffy took a deep shot very early and barely overthrew star wideout Stephen Smalls, who was open. Smalls pulled a hamstring on the play and was, crucially, done for the night. The first half was otherwise all defense — violent, physical defense. It was 0-0 at halftime.

Then the Barons put together a third quarter for the ages in terms of resourcefulness and big-game polish. Williams surprised CV coach Gerad Novak by taking the wind at his back in the third quarter. Central scored on its first three second-half possessions, all on very short fields, thanks to a fumble recovery and two bad into-the-wind punts. At the end of the third quarter, Williams called time with 0:00 showing on the scoreboard clock because he knew three seconds still remained on the official clock kept by the referee on the field. That forced another wind-stuffed CV punt, another short field and, a few minutes later, another touchdown. It was 28-0, and Central's four touchdown drives averaged just 33 yards. Without Smalls, CV was limited to Steffy trying to make something happen out of the shotgun, play after play after play. He completed 10 of 17 passes, but for just 5 yards per attempt. The Buckskins ran for only 88 yards, many of them by Steffy scrambling in desperation. What was a defensive battle for three of four quarters ended up a semi-blowout on the scoreboard. The Barons had clinched the Section Two title, and the top seed in the District Three AAA playoffs.

Although that was the symbolic end of the regular season, Central blasted overmatched Solanco 61-0 a week later. Central had outscored its opponents 405-40, outgained them by 403 yards per game to 190. No individual Baron was among the top 15 rushers, or top 25 receivers, or even top 10 point-scorers in the Lancaster-Lebanon League. None of which surprised anyone in the Central camp. They really were a team. They expected to be 10-0, and saw the regular season as a means to a much bigger end. "We knew we were pretty good," Byrne said. "The coaches kept us grounded. In our minds, we wanted to run the table."

Chapter 6:
The Playoffs

That the Barons held the top seed in the District Three playoffs was no better news for Central than the No. 2 seeding of Lower Dauphin, which had stunned them in the semis the previous season. The Falcons' only loss was a 27-8 upset at Hershey in Week 7. Lower Dauphin thus shared the Mid-Penn Conference Capital Division title with Hershey, which was coming to Elden Rettew Stadium for a district semi. The venue itself was news: District Three had decided to play first-round district games at the higher seed's field for the first time.

It was important news to Wilt, rehabbing fanatically but watching practices and games from the sidelines in frustration for the past three weeks. "No way I was missing my last chance to play on our field," he said. By Thursday of game week, Wilt had convinced Central's trainers to agree that if he could run pass routes and catch the ball at more-or-less full speed and with manageable pain, they'd clear him to play. He did it, the trainers themselves making the throws. "It was brutal," he said. "I was in so much pain it was unbelievable, but I pretended I wasn't. I just had to suck it up."

The game was less suspenseful. Williams, who had been gradually easing the reins on Hunter, now turned

> *"It was brutal ... I was in so much pain it was unbelievable, but I pretended I wasn't. I just had to suck it up."*
>
> **Shawn Wilt**

Opposite page:
Baron fans
celebrate a
blowout of
Lower Dauphin
for the district
championship.

Tyler McCauley smothered Shamokin's Rich Schiccatano for a
safety, above; Jarryd Moyer threw for four touchdowns and ran
for two, below.

In the district final versus Lower Dauphin, Jarryd Moyer, right, had room to roam. His counterpart, Matt Ruffner, above, did not.

him loose. He ran for 196 yards in 15 tries — about 13 yards per carry — including a 78-yard touchdown. "That sucker ran wild on us," said Bob "Gump" May, Hershey's grizzled ex-Marine coach. "He's only a sophomore? That's scary." Eric Meyers went for 101 yards in 14 carries, and Central piled up 390 yards on the ground. It wasn't as close as the 35-15 final suggested. Shawn Wilt? They didn't let him play defense, but he got his feet wet, catching two passes for 41 yards.

Lower Dauphin, meanwhile, eased past West Perry, 31-14, in the other semi. The Falcons still featured quarterback Matt Ruffner, who was brilliant in the 2002 game and had thrown the touchdown pass at the final gun to win it. Lower Dauphin was well-coached and comfortable in the postseason. Also, its fans would surely argue, the Falcons had played better competition in the Mid-Penn. It was a pretty weak argument. The teams had three common opponents, Elizabethtown, Middletown and Hershey. Lower Dauphin was 2-1 in those games with an aggregate score of 55-51. That's 55 for the other guys. Manheim Central had pounded those three by a combined 108-15.

There was a script to the 2003 district final, and the Barons had memorized it. Its theme was defense. Lower Dauphin never got within 30 yards of Central's goal line. It never crossed the 50-yard line before halftime, at which point the score was 24-0 and the game was effectively over. The Falcons ran 29 times for 30 yards. Ruffner completed 12 of 19 throws, but for only 74 yards. He was hounded mercilessly, thrown to the turf often and had two of his team's four lost fumbles. The final was 38-0 and, again, it wasn't that close. It was Central's 13th championship, and 11th in 12 years. The Barons had lost one district playoff game in 14 tries, and now they had, if not erased that loss, certainly avenged it. They were supposed to win districts, of course. It was the nature of things that Central's season, or at least the part that would define it, hadn't even started yet.

Shamokin, Central's opponent in the first round of state playoffs, was part of a rich football history in Pennsylvania's coal region. But the style of play, even as recently as 2003, was stereotypically from the 1950s, little more than straightforward running, blocking and tackling. In 1999, 2000 and 2001, Central had faced Coal Region opponents in the first round of the state playoffs (quarterfinals) and had thrown at them an array of offenses they clearly had not seen before, outscoring them by a combined 129-49. Berwick was an exception to all of that, of course, but perhaps an exception that proved the rule.

Shamokin was supposed to be different. The Indians had gotten there with defense. After they held Selinsgrove to 78 yards and forcing seven turnovers in a 47-8 romp in the District Four championship the previous week, Selinsgrove coach Bill Grove said, "It seems like they have 15 guys on the field. Shamokin's

defense is like 11 hungry dogs going after one bone." Media coverage in the run-up to the game focused on the matchup between Central's offense and Shamokin's D to the exclusion — the unfair exclusion, Williams thought — of Central's defense. That gave him a chance to do something he always enjoyed: read press clippings to his team, then pin them on the locker room wall. Williams found more intangibles he liked when the Barons arrived at the venue, the 7,200-seat Silver Bowl at Mount Carmel High School. Like Berwick, Mount Carmel was an exception to the Coal Region stereotype, with five state AA titles in the trophy case, all since 1994. "Very impressive," Williams said. There was the agreeably gritty atmosphere of the Silver Bowl, set ostentatiously in the middle of Mount Carmel, surrounded by a graveyard, a grocery store, a bar and an assisted-living facility.

Shamokin could indeed defend the hell out of the run, but it did so by rolling all 11 defenders to within a yard of the line of scrimmage, which might have been overkill. Williams scripted Central's first 10 offensive plays with play-action passing in mind. Jarryd Moyer took the game's first snap from the shotgun and was instantly sacked. The teams traded punts until Jeremy Smith got off a great one that settled at the Shamokin 3-yard line. One snap later, Tyler McCauley smothered Shamokin's Rich Schiccatano for an easy safety, and the Barons were off. Moyer had quietly evolved into a big-time

Opposite page: Craig Gatchell fends off Shamokin's Kenny Etzel, top; and Mike Williams addresses the offense during a time-out, below.

Eric Meyers, right, tries to break the tackle of Hershey's David Bennett.

quarterback and was being recruited by Division I-AA colleges such as Delaware, where Matt Nagy had played. Quietly, because so much attention had
been paid all season to the offensive line, the defense, Hunter and the ground
game. But now, with an opponent crowding the line and daring Moyer to make
plays, he more than delivered. A strike to Ryan Dennes, who was so well-
covered that it had to be a strike, made it 16-0. A deep-post throw laid perfectly
in Dennes' arms made it 23-0. Moyer finished the game completing nine of 12
passes for 164 yards, or nearly 14 yards per attempt, and four touchdowns, with
no turnovers. He also ran for two scores.

The most remarkable thing about Moyer's performance was how unneces-
sary it turned out to be. Central's defense had painted another masterpiece. The
Indians wouldn't have scored if the game had been a week long. They managed
60 yards and five first downs. The final, which became official long after a caravan of Central fans had started down the mountain on Interstate 81, was 50-0.
The Barons were two wins from the end of the rainbow, as far as any Central
team had ever been. Ghosts of Decembers past loomed, and an old tormentor
was up next.

> *"I remember they brought in space heaters for practice, and I remember the quarterbacks hanging around them between snaps."*
>
> Kevin Krause

Chapter 7:
Strath Haven

Post-Thanksgiving football in Pennsylvania meant a couple things: When almost no one else was still playing, you still were; and if you intended to keep playing, you were going to have to win in bad weather. "It seemed like it was freezing at practice almost every night," Kevin Krause recalled. "I remember they brought in space heaters for practice, and I remember the quarterbacks hanging around them between snaps." Strath Haven had won eight straight District One AAA titles, and played for the state championship the previous four years, winning it all in 1999 and 2001. The Panthers' 2003 season was, if anything, more dominant than Central's. They were undefeated, had outscored their opponents 528-55 and had rushed for more than 4,000 yards. They were the top-ranked AAA team in the state. Central was second.

Strath Haven operated almost exclusively out of the Wing-T, a fullback-intensive, ground-oriented offense still popular in the high school game, even though long since outmoded at higher levels. Dan Connor, the Panthers' star fullback/linebacker, had been a first-team all-state choice as a junior and was already committed to Penn State. Connor was 6-3, 220 and ran a 4.5-second 40-yard dash. He had rushed for 1,750 yards and 28 touchdowns that season, and was better at linebacker, a position he would play at Penn State and then in the NFL. Strath Haven, at least by reputation, played the kind of simple power football that holds up in winter. Central, at least by reputation, did it more with finesse and dazzle. "They have a very multiple offense for high school," Strath Haven coach Kevin Clancy told the Intell's Ed Gruver during game week. It was a compliment, but in Pennsylvania after Thanksgiving, a diverse playbook

Coach Williams and his staff understood the hurdle the Barons had finally cleared.

could be superfluous.

Then there was the hardest of hard facts: Central was 0-8 at this stage of the playoffs. The Barons practiced on Thanksgiving morning. Jeff Smoker, home from Michigan State, spoke to the team afterward. "You know what's on the line," he told them. "All I can tell you to do is to make the most of it. Make sure this isn't your last game." On Friday, the Barons gathered at a Manheim church to watch "Remember the Titans," a film starring Denzel Washington that was one of Williams' favorites, a sort of football version of "Hoosiers."

There were some issues, heading into the showdown on a Saturday afternoon at Coatesville High School. One, it rained torrentially most of the day Friday, which rendered the field at Coatesville, already battered by a full football season, a muddy mess. Two, a flu bug ran through the Barons during the week. Triple-figure temperatures were all over the place. None of them would miss the game (as if it was ever a possibility), but many of them felt badly enough to be, potentially, less than their optimal selves. Jarryd Moyer spiked at 102 and received a shot Friday night and another one Saturday morning. "After that, I was good," he said. "I really wasn't nervous at all."

Then there was the cleat controversy. Williams had heard from a District One source that Strath Haven was among a number of District One teams that used too-long, illegal cleats on muddy fields. "It wasn't anything I had even heard of before," Williams said. "I thought, when the teams come out, let's check it out." When the Panthers hit the field for warm-ups, Williams said, "Connor looked like he was 6-7." Williams called the officials over. He told them he didn't want to penalize anybody, didn't want to get anybody in trouble, but … "I think the other team has illegal cleats on." So the refs set to work, measuring cleats for both teams. Thirty Strath Haven players were illegal. No Barons were. As it hap-

After the Strath Haven game, it didn't seem that cold to Jarryd Moyer and two young fans.

pened — and Williams knew this going in — Coatesville had extra, legal cleats
to outfit the Panthers. "It was a bit of a scramble," Williams said. "(Clancy) is a
friend, and I didn't want to upset him. Whether it disrupted their pregame routine, I don't know." Williams wasn't smiling at all as he said that.

Cleats weren't decisive, but the conditions were horrendous. The temperature hovered right around freezing, but winds of 45 mph made the thermometer
seem satirical. This is how cold it was: At halftime, Central kicker Ryan Plowman decided — sensibly for a kicker — to sacrifice his hands for his feet and
try to stuff hand warmers between his toes. His hands were frozen so stiff and
unlimber that it took him the entire halftime break to get his cleats off and on.
The conditions created a remarkable game, football as it must have been played
a century before, a land-acquisition game on a miniature scale. The only way to
play this game was the way Strath Haven always played. On this day, Central
did it better.

Williams rarely ventured off the first page of the playbook. On defense, the
Barons changed from their usual 4-3 front to a 5-2, with Krause at noseguard.
Brubaker sometimes made that adjustment against two-tight-end fronts. "We
had some push up front," Krause said. "I thought it was evident pretty early we
had the better defense." The hitting was savage, much of it involving Connor,
much of it within a body length of the middle of the line of scrimmage. "It was
exciting to go against Connor," Byrne said. "It was a personal challenge. I remember some violent collisions with him."

First downs were
like points. Central piled
up 11 of them before
halftime, Hunter, Mey-
ers and Moyer hauling
the mail, the line hauling
ass. Early in the second
quarter, on fourth down
at the Strath Haven 18-
yard line, Williams called
for the field-goal team
to attempt a 25-yarder
into the wind. Plowman's

**When it was over, the
Barons could barely
feel the cold.**

Jeremiha Hunter pounded out 115 critical yards.

reaction: "Are you kidding me?" In pregame warm-ups, Plowman did not make a kick, from any distance, on that end of the field. Every single one he tried blew back at him, or went wildly to one side or the other. "I had no doubt I was going to miss," Plowman recalled.

"I figured I was going to end up on my butt, with the ball blown back in my face. But, I just kept my head down and did my thing." Somehow it worked. "Nobody talks about that," Krause said, "but it still blows my mind that Plowman made that field goal." Plowman was a multisport athlete who technically ended up the only 2003 Central senior to play major-college football, since he spent a year as a walk-on backup kicker at the University of Pittsburgh. But he was really a soccer guy and had never played football before 2003. That kick, he says now, helped get him into the fraternity. "It wasn't the easiest thing, coming from the soccer world," he said. "After the Strath Haven game, I got let in a little bit more."

"I had no doubt I was going to miss. I figured I was going to end up on my butt, with the ball blown back in my face. But, I just kept my head down and did my thing."

Ryan Plowman

That made it 3-0 at halftime, leading to Williams' locker-room choice on the wind, followed by his prayer, but really inspired by his ultimate faith in his defense. In the third quarter, Williams went for a fourth-and-2 from his own 11 rather than punt into the wind. The Barons' first punt of the game came soon after, still into the wind. It went 5 yards. Strath Haven took over at the Central 39. Connor rumbled for 9 yards. The Panthers got 2 yards, and a first down, over three jarring plays. Shawn Wilt promptly intercepted Strath Haven QB Rick Coppick. Moments later, the third quarter ended. Central would have the wind the rest of the way. Strath Haven had the ball at its own 33-yard line with 5:32 left. Coppick hit Connor on a third-and-9 swing pass, and finally the Big Gun had some running room. Connor got the first down, then into Central territory. Then Craig Gatchell hit Connor and separated him from the ball. "Trying to make something happen," Connor admitted, "I lost focus."

"The ball was just bouncing along," Wilt recalled, "right in front of me." Wilt fell on it. Jeremy Smith fell on Wilt. "I held on like my life depended on it," Wilt said. "I curled up around it like it was a baby." The game wasn't over, but it was starting to feel like it. Meyers, terrific in traffic all day, lashed up the middle to convert a third-and-6. Hunter, who finished with 115 yards, dragged Panthers seven yards. Nate Mast moved the chains on his only carry of the day. Moyer went nine yards, and then Hunter moved the chains. This was as elemental as football gets: Push the other guys back. Push the ball down the field. It was only 3-0, but on the line of scrimmage, Central was closing in on a knockout. Then Moyer was taking a knee, the clock was running away and it was over.

There's no such thing as a 3-0 blowout, but this was decisive. Central had 239 yards and 15 first downs. Strath Haven had 80 and eight. "They just out-manned us," said a gracious Connor. "They're on a mission." Clancy was equally gracious. "That's the best line we played against all year," he said. "We've run the ball well all year, and today we couldn't."

Some games in '03 belonged to Hunter, or to Moyer, or to the defense; this one belonged, more than anyone else, to Byrne, the trench anchor, whom Connor called "a great, great player." "We just pounded the ball the whole game," Byrne said. "It was a fun game, now that I think about it." Central had scaled the wall. In its ninth attempt, the program finally had a win in the state semifinals. Six days later, it would play in the sport's ultimate game. On the bus home, there was no delirium. There was mostly silence, as the flu-ridden Barons slept.

Opposite page: Fans welcome Jarryd Moyer and the Barons back to Manheim.

"Headlights kindled a halo around the buses. Dozens of car horns ripped the chilly air."

Jon Rutter
Sunday News reporter

Chapter 8:
Championship Week

It was evening by the time Manheim Central's team bus got back to town. Crowds lined Hershey Avenue in front of the school, Sunday News reporter Jon Rutter among them. "Headlights kindled a halo around the buses. Dozens of car horns ripped the chilly air," Rutter wrote. Williams spent much of Saturday night taking congratulatory calls, one of them from Paul Fixter, coach

of the American Hockey League Hershey Bears, minutes after the Bears had defeated Norfolk. Fixter described his team's win as "fulfilling." He described Central's win as "awesome." Fixter, who had won a Stanley Cup as an assistant coach with the Colorado Avalanche, was friendly with Williams. "Big day (in Manheim)," Fixter said. "I've met Mike before. I went and spoke to (the team). … Talked about championships and winning. I loved it."

As influenza among the Central players eased, Baron fever was bordering on epidemic in Manheim and beyond. Two related worries focused the players and coaches amid the hoopla: 1) avoiding letdown and 2) nobody knew anything about Pine-Richland. For Central, this time of year meant Berwick, or Strath Haven, Allentown Central Catholic. But Pine-Richland? Not a brand name. In a story in the Nov. 16 Sunday News, Williams had praised the depth of talent in the AAA state tournament field, mentioning, among others, Shamokin and Thomas Jefferson, an emerging power from suburban Pittsburgh. No mention of Pine-Richland, which would handle Thomas Jefferson 27-7 a week later. In the state semis, the Rams romped over Bradford, 37-7. "Just their being WPIAL was something," Williams said. "We felt … dismayed, I guess, by how much those teams bragged about their football. And I remember hearing about this wide receiver they had who was a great baseball player. That was about all I knew."

Customer Susan Lease, left, and cashier Doni Lefever show off paraphernalia featuring their favorite high school football team at Longenecker's True Value in Manheim.

Evan Earhart, left, and Mark Murr, of the Manheim Twin Kiss, believed in dinner specials and the Barons.

Clair Altemus, P-R's veteran coach, wasn't sure about the Rams in the summer of 2003. The previous year's team reached the WPIAL Class AAA final, where it lost to Hopewell in an epic game. It was the Rams' best season in decades, and 14 senior starters returned, including Neil Walker, the wideout Williams mentioned. In baseball, Walker was considered the country's top high school catcher, a probable first-round pick in the June Major League Baseball draft. Altemus' concern was at quarterback, where the best one he'd ever coached, Kevin McCabe, had graduated to the University of Virginia. "We didn't even have a solid backup," Altemus said.

Walker was less than a year away from either turning pro in baseball or taking a scholarship offer from Clemson. He would be away all summer for baseball, including representing the United States in the Pan-Am Games. He didn't really want to play QB, but Altemus met with Walker and his father and talked them into it anyway, at least tentatively. "They were both whatever's-best-for-the-team guys," Altemus said. Enter Jake Long, a sophomore who transferred from Bradford. Long had played some as a freshman on a state playoff team, but in a run-dominated Wing-T offense. Inflated roster stats aside, Long was only about 5-10, 160 pounds. Altemus was dubious, but Long would get a shot, especially with Walker away. In his first 7-on-7 scrimmage, Long flawlessly zinged four touchdown passes. "I said, I guess we have a guy who can guide the bug-

With Central one win from a coveted state title, Manheim was caught up in the excitement.

gy," Altemus said. "I guess we can move Walker back to receiver. People still ac-
cuse me of foul play. They still think I must have recruited the kid, but I didn't.
His dad really did get transferred here." The Rams didn't quite have the size
and strength of Manheim Central, but they had everything else. With a superb
collection of skill-position players, they may have been sneaking up on people.
Undefeated, they had outscored their opponents 513-125 through 14 games.

On Monday, coaches from the two staffs hit the Pennsylvania Turnpike and
met at the Breezewood exit, roughly halfway between Pittsburgh and Manheim,
to exchange film. Neither coach saw anything daunting. "When we saw them on
film, we knew they were good, but it wasn't like they were overwhelming," Williams said. "I think we felt pretty confident we could win." Altemus was pretty
confident, too. "I knew they were big … I knew we'd have to finesse them," he
said. "I knew they were well-coached because they didn't make mistakes."

Later in the week came a third worry: the weather, again. By Wednesday
night, the National Weather Service was tracking a storm coming from the Mis-
sissippi River Valley, and a second storm, then in Tennessee. Both were bringing
snow, sleet and wind, and were expected to arrive in Hershey the same time
as the Barons and Rams, Friday night. Low temperatures Friday evening were
predicted to be around 25 degrees. FieldTurf, a state-of-the-art playing surface,
had been installed at Hersheypark Stadium that year. "I was apprehensive about
the weather, but the field was artificial turf," Altemus said. "I thought on a good
surface, we could stay with them."

There was little apprehension in Manheim. A sign on The Caddy Shack, a
restaurant and miniature-golf course in Manheim, announced that it would
be closed Friday: "Going to See Barons Become State Champ." The storefront
window at Tanner Chiropractic on Main Street had a mannequin getting a back
adjustment. And wearing a Manheim Central helmet. Manheim Mennonite
Church had an oddly serious message: "Yesterday's hits won't win today's ball-
game."

On Wednesday, the Lancaster-Lebanon League held its annual football banquet, at which Central players took 11 of a possible 30 spots with the all-Section
Two first-team offense, defense and specialists. Moyer at quarterback and linemen Byrne, Trovato and Neil Hershey made the offense. The defense included
linemen Krause, Neil Hershey (with Ephrata running back Rock, the only
two-way first-teamers) and Kevin Hershey, linebacker Hunter, safety Wilt and
cornerback Dennes. Among the specialists was punter Smith. Moyer was named
outstanding back of the year. Byrne was lineman, and offensive lineman, of the
year. Krause was defensive lineman of the year. All nice honors. And given the
timing and context, barely a footnote.

Chapter 9:

The Game

$\mathbf{M}$anheim Central didn't have school Friday due to the weather. The players, some of them still recovering from the flu and all of them teenagers, mostly slept in. Many of the seniors gathered, as they often did, at Shawn Wilt's house in town, not far from school. "His mom cooked legendary food," Kevin Krause said. It was already snowing and, by some forecasts, the worst was hours away. Coach Williams didn't think there was any way they would play the game, but by 2 p.m. the players at Wilt's house were watching the Class A state final in progress on TV between Southern Columbia and Bishop Carroll, and eventually they headed over to the locker room.

There had already been weather-related machinations. Pine-Richland had not trav-

During time-outs, crews did their best to keep the field clear.

The play that won it: Shawn Wilt blocks Patrick Humes' overtime extra point.

"All I was thinking was, we've got to get there. Well, I was also thinking, I can't believe they're still playing this game."

Mike Williams

eled to Hershey the night before. That was Coach Altemus' call. "Young kids in a hotel, they won't sleep. All kinds of stupid stuff could happen," he said. It's about a four-hour drive, more than 200 miles, from Pittsburgh to Hershey. The Rams loaded themselves and their equipment in a bus and got ready to head east. It was snowing in Pitts-burgh, and not lightly. Only then did Altemus, who was also P-R's athletic director, join a conference call with George Derbyshire, Central's longtime athletic director; Robert Lombardi, then the PIAA's associate director and co-chairman; and PIAA Executive Director Brad Cashman. Looking back, Altemus said Derbyshire didn't want to play. "I said we're all loaded up, we're coming," Altemus said. "As close (to Hershey) as they were, they could start walking now and get there. I don't know if I came across as crass or if I was just being an idiot." Neither Derbyshire nor Lombardi recall it being quite that clear-cut. "There were a number of options," Lombardi said. "When (Pine-Richland) said they wanted to play, I was good with it."

"I was all for playing the next day, I guess," Derbyshire said. "But they had the longer, more dangerous trip. I put the ball in their court." The upshot of the conference call was that the teams would meet at the stadium that night and, unless intervening weather made it unworkable, the game would be played.

Mike Williams saved some plays for overtime, top.

Greg Hough was a handful for the Central defense, right.

Once the Rams' got east of Pittsburgh on the Pennsylvania Turnpike, the sun started shining. They stopped in Breezewood to stretch and get some food. Soon after they got back on the bus, it started snowing. The closer they got to Hershey, the harder it snowed. P-R officials on the bus called home and canceled the bus scheduled to bring the band to the game.

Central's players were gathering in the school's locker room, where they got a kick out of reading good-luck letters from students at Manheim Central elementary schools. There was snow on the ground, but the roads were still drivable. About 4 p.m., the Barons loaded up for the 7 p.m. game and headed to Hershey, normally a 25- or 30-minute drive via Routes 72 and 322. But just a few minutes out of Manheim, near the Lebanon-Lancaster turnpike exchange, an accident blocked Route 72.

The bus and the equipment truck trailing it, driven by Derbyshire, were stopped dead with the clock ticking. "All I was thinking was, we've got to get there," Williams said. "Well, I was also thinking, I can't believe they're still playing this game." He called the PIAA and let them know they were stuck in traffic. Then Williams directed the bus to get on the turnpike, drive to the Harrisburg East exit 19 miles to the west, and enter Hershey from the other side. Except for Williams ("I always panic"), there was apparently minimal anxiety on the bus. Meyers always took a nap on the ride to road games, usually waking up just as the bus pulled into the stadium. Now he woke up on the turnpike. "All I thought was, where are we?" he said.

> *"It was amazing how running backs kept getting extra yards. It was so hard to wrap up, and after a while you got conscious of that."*
>
> Mike Byrne

It took Central two hours to get there. When the Barons arrived, Williams figured, "they'll kinda move everything back a little, give us some time." Nope. The normal pregame routine in football is a full-blown warm-up, including passing and catching and kicking, followed by a return to the locker room, and then charging back on the field a few minutes before the game starts. For Central in 2003, the ritual included blasting Phil Collins' "In the Air Tonight" after returning to the locker room. The only thing in the air was snow. For the biggest game possible, it was another detail compromised. "We got there, got dressed, warmed up a little, and that was it," Moyer said. "We never went back in. That was the only disappointing thing."

It was snowing steadily at kickoff. Swirling winds sporadically created blizzardlike conditions and made the air seem much colder than the temperature, which was around 30 degrees. The weather changed everything, and not in

Shawn Wilt lies in the end zone after scoring an overtime touchdown.

ways you'd expect. The hardest thing to do wasn't throwing or catching; it was open-field tackling. Especially on a dead run, it seemed nearly impossible to do the usual plant-and-drive thing to bring down a ball carrier. "It was amazing how running backs kept getting extra yards," Byrne said. "It was so hard to wrap up, and after a while you got conscious of that." Early in the game, Krause was wrestling Long down for a sack, and Byrne, believing no tackle was safe, came in late and drilled Long for an obvious late-hit penalty. "It was really blatant," Byrne said. "(Krause) still hounds me about that."

It was the same for everybody, of course. If anything, it added to the drama. There were nine offensive plays of 40 yards or more, including a 91-yard kickoff return, a 72-yard punt return, and pass plays of 65 and 55 yards. It was soon clear that, with Long and Walker and running back Greg Hough, Pine-Richland had by far the most skilled and explosive group of runners and throwers and catchers the Barons had faced. But Pine-Richland led only 9-3 at halftime.

Central had scored first, with Plowman hitting from 27 yards out. But Hough returned the ensuing kickoff 91 yards for a touchdown. The extra point, by P-R kicker Patrick Humes, sailed wide right. The Rams blocked a punt late in the half, taking over at the Central 16, but the Barons held, then blocked a 23-yard field goal try. Pine-Richland did something unusual on field goals and PATs: Instead of a standard alignment with one wing player on each side of the line, a yard behind scrimmage to protect against kick-blocks, the Rams put two

wings on the same side, with the holder and kicker shading to that side, pre-
sumably to cut down the angle of the kick. Brubaker noticed it on film. "You'd
think people would be able to take advantage of that," he said. Yeah, you'd
think.

Ryan Dennes, just 5 feet 10 inches tall and 170 pounds but arguably the most
underrated Baron, started the second-half dramatics with a brilliant punt return
for a 73-yard touchdown. Long, who somehow seemed more comfortable gripping and throwing the ball in the weather than Moyer, quickly answered with
a 55-yard TD strike to tight end Billy Massaro. Then the Rams stopped Central,
but roughed the punter. In a game spectacularly free of mistakes, P-R made
more critical ones. Hunter promptly went 45 yards to the Rams' 1-yard line, and
scored a play later. Central thus took an 18-15 lead to the final quarter.

At every stoppage, crews would run on the field with shovels, clearing each
5-yard line as much as possible. The conditions were worsening as the game
wore on, but it happened gradually and somewhat sporadically, so that it's hard
a decade later to see a specific point where calling it would have made sense. Especially because of what was happening on the field. "We never really thought
of that," Lombardi said. "Obviously, the quality of play wasn't being affected."

Early in the fourth, Hough gathered in a Long pass and slalomed 65 yards
through the Barons for another TD. Hough ran for 126 yards, plus that reception and a 91-yard kickoff return. He was among several kids — dozens, maybe
— playing the game of his life. It was starting to look as if the Rams had more
weapons. It was even starting to look like the weather was to their advantage.
"The advantage is always to the offense in conditions like that," Byrne said, looking back. "Who knows what would have happened in a fair-weather game? I'd
like to think our offensive and defensive lines would have been the difference."

It was 25-22 in favor of Pine-Richland in the final stanza, Central taking
over on their own 17, the wind and snow seemingly at their howling worst. The
Barons promptly jumped before the snap: first-and-15, 88 yards away. Central
got nothing on first down, nothing on second. Then Moyer drilled a big-time
throw through the blizzard, hitting Dennes for 42 yards. The drive was long and
relentless. On fourth-and-1 from the 11, Hunter got the yard. Moyer and Byrne
botched the next exchange under center — the first time, Moyer said, that had
happened all year. Soon it was fourth-and-10, the clock nearing the five-minute
mark. Central called time.

Back under center, Moyer said he remembered not liking what he saw
before the snap, but he just went with it. He danced in the pocket, no one open,
then scrambled, and scrambled some more, almost ghostlike in the particularly dark, gloomy north end of the stadium. Then he let the ball go, creating
the play that turned the game from merely great to surreal. Two Rams, one of

Pine-Richland might have won it in regulation, had Shawn Wilt not broken up this pass to Neil Walker.

them Walker, dove, their bodies parallel to the ground, and missed breaking up the pass by what seemed like fractions of an inch. The ball hit the numbers of Central receiver Ryan Huber in the end zone. He cradled it. It was only his sixth catch of the year. It was like something from a Disney film. The play, in retrospect, seems bigger and more decisive than it was, with 4:58 still remaining and Pine-Richland so loaded with playmakers.

Long hit Walker for 32 yards to the Central 41. Then Hough ran four straight times, to the 14. But here Central rose up, with Wilt brilliantly breaking up a pass to Walker in the end zone. The Rams would try a field goal, to tie it, with a minute left. The kicker, Humes, had been wobbly. This was no chip shot from 31 yards. But with the season on the line, kicking in what amounted to Siberia, Humes drilled it.

Play on. Snow on, blow on and play on. "It seemed like we could be here forever, scoring back and forth," Moyer said. Coach Altemus said later that if you had asked him to predict this, he'd have said you were out of your mind.

Williams had scripted plays for two overtimes. Those plays included a package he had kept under wraps until then, featuring Moyer rolling to his right and making a play. The Rams scored first, on Walker's 7-yard run. Central matched, with Moyer rolling on a keeper for 10 yards to the 1. Craig Gatchell took it in from there. In the second overtime, Central went first, scoring when Moyer rolled again and found Wilt. Pine-Richland answered on four straight Hough runs, as newspaper deadlines dissolved in the cold.

Now it was getting very late, and the snow was piling up. Understandably, very few of the roughly 5,000 fans had left. The PIAA honchos, Lombardi and Cashman, may or may not have considered calling the game at this point, declaring the team's co-champions. Altemus said that's exactly what he was told was about to happen, at a banquet a year later. Mike Clair, Central's longtime statistician, says he thought he heard Cashman and Lombardi discussing it on the sidelines. Lombardi says it never happened. Cashman is now retired and was unavailable for comment. Williams says he's glad they never came to him with the option. "Everybody says there's no way I'd have accepted that, if I had the choice," he said. "How do you know? To me, it would have been a logical decision. ... You have the chance to be a state champ, or play on and possibly come in second? I don't know what I would have done."

All that was contingent, of course, on Humes making the extra point. As they shoveled the field to prepare for the kick, Clair said he overheard the head linesman saying to one of his crewmates, "They're going to block this." The official had apparently heard some of the Central kids cooking up a plan on their own. That was news to Williams, who was hard at work putting play-calls together for a third overtime. And perhaps a fourth or fifth.

Wilt still remembers the play as if it had happened five minutes before. "We had blocked one earlier, so they doubled on the block side," he said. "Hunter and Smith switched sides pre-snap. Hunter was supposed to run to the left, and I was supposed to cover the tight end, but our extra man, Smith, ran over opposite (the tight end)." It created just a bit of confusion on the P-R side. Ryan Dennes, a defensive back, stepped up to the line of scrimmage, Wilt said, so the Barons had a 4-on-3. Pre-snap, Wilt smacked Smith on his shoulder pads and yelled, "Take him out," meaning the wing on the overloaded side. Wilt was the odd man, with no Ram to occupy him. On the snap, he remembers stepping over the legs of two jousting linemen and flying straight to the ball. He laid out and … a routine play became a spectacular one. A decisive one. A historic one.

Manheim Central 39, Pine-Richland 38.

> *"Do we know how to throw a parade, or what? Naked guys and tubas!"*
>
> Pat Houck
> Manheim resident

Chapter 10:
The Aftermath

Some players, in the frenzy, didn't immediately realize the game was over. It didn't seem right, or at least clear. "I was running to recover the ball," Kevin Krause said. "Then somebody ran into me, and I woke up." Just before the extra point, after the P-R touchdown, Brian Hunter had slumped over, hands on knees. "I was so cold," he said. "I didn't think I could take it anymore." After the block, he said, it was suddenly 95 degrees. "I took my jacket off." Mike Clair said it all seemed to happen in slow motion. "People were jumping up and down and moving, but they really didn't know that they were jumping about for a while. It was hard for it to sink in."

And then it did. Manheim Central players were flopping on their backs and making angels in the ever-thickening snow. Greg

Reality sank in fast – the Barons were state champs.

Conti, a 270-pound Pine-Richland lineman who had played heroically, held on to one of his coaches with both arms and wept in agony. Soon Williams, holding a trophy, was being carried by his players and looking

"It might have been the best speech I've ever heard. It was emotional, but it connected with everybody. It turned everything into a positive, made everyone feel better. I wish to God I'd taped it."

Clair Altemus

iconic. The Barons did delirious interviews, hugged their delirious families and friends. "This is the most exciting thing that's happened in my life," Jarryd Moyer said.

Central coach Mike Williams spoke for everyone. "I'm just amazed at the things high school kids are able to do." The final numbers don't do these things justice. They do, if lamely, tell part of the story. Greg Hough had 370 all-purpose yards, but Neil Walker didn't go nuts, just four rushes and two catches for 76 yards. Hunter had 99 yards in 15 rushes, Meyers 72 in 16. Pine-Richland had more yards (344, a monstrous number against Central's defense) and more first downs. Central had more time of possession, fewer penalties and zero turnovers (to P-R's one). Central made fewer mistakes, especially in the kicking game. Wilt revealed a couple days later that he had suffered a concussion when he took a hit in the back of the neck in the third quarter. He was in pain, and his mind foggy, much of the rest of the game. Given today's head-trauma protocols, he probably wouldn't have been in there at the end.

"I'm just amazed at the things high school kids are able to do."

Mike Williams

The Pine-Richland locker room was painfully silent. Much had been made of Central's history of agonizing near-misses, but the year before, the Rams had run out of time 2 yards from the winning score in the state semifinal. And now this. Outside the locker room, Altemus called his young staff together. "Get your ass in there and hug every one of those kids," he told them. "Tell 'em what they mean to us. It took a while, but we made sure we did that." Still, the short bus ride to the hotel was very subdued. When they arrived, they found that parents had set up a buffet and formed a human tunnel all the way from the bus to the food. "I wanted to cry out of disbelief," Altemus said. "They must've blown 10 grand. But when the kids started shoveling food in themselves, I think everybody started to feel a little better."

At length — considerable length — the Barons piled into the bus and pulled out of Hershey with the gold. They were greeted in Manheim with a police escort and, at the school, a crowd of more than 500. The lateness of the hour,

**The blocked PAT
was followed by a
wild celebration.**

and the weather, put
some damper on the
celebrating that night
or, more accurately,
spread it out over the
coming days. The Rams
drove home the follow-
ing morning. As they rode, Altemus felt a hand on his shoulder. It was Walker,
who whispered that he wanted to say something. Altemus nodded, and Walker
turned to address his teammates. "It might have been the best speech I've ever
heard," Altemus said. "It was emotional, but it connected with everybody. It
turned everything into a positive, made everyone feel better. I wish to God I'd
taped it."

For several years, Altemus said, a
Pittsburgh-area TV station replayed
the game around the holidays. Did he
watch? "No," he said. "I know how it
comes out." For the same reason, in
Manheim they watched it over and
over. Wilt and Williams both said they
had seen the entire broadcast four or
five times by the time Manheim held its
parade and formal festivities, nine days
after the game. There was a celebration
at the school, for Central students only,
that Sunday afternoon. Then Williams,
sitting in a red '69 Mercury Cougar
convertible, led a procession toward the
town square, followed by the obligatory
shirtless fans with letters spelling "Barons" on their chests. (The temperature

The Barons received pro-style championship rings.

was a modest 37.) Then came the band, followed by the players and cheerleaders on flatbed trucks, tossing candy into the crowd lining the street. After the parade, back at the school, there were food and autograph sessions, with T-shirts and other memorabilia for sale. Everyone watched the game one more time on a huge-screen TV. "Do we know how to throw a parade, or what?" Manheim resident Pat Houck told the Intell. "Naked guys and tubas!"

The following week, The Associated Press all-state teams were announced. Moyer and Byrne made the first team. So did Pine-Richland's Walker, Conti and Hough. Hunter made the second team. Dan Connor was the Class AAA Player of the Year. The AAA coach of the year, naturally, was Williams.

A few weeks later, at a meeting of the Manheim Central school board, President Terry Hackman read a letter from Joseph Lalli, athletic director at Scranton Prep, and a football official who had worked the Strath Haven game. Lalli wrote to congratulate the Barons on their season and, in particular, Williams, for what Lalli called "the greatest act of sportsmanship on a football field that I have ever witnessed." Something about illegal cleats.

Mike Williams leads the parade with his assistants Dave Hahn, back left, and John Brubaker.

*"This is the most
exciting thing
that's happened in
my life."*

Jarryd Moyer

**Manheim's formal
celebration wasn't until
nine days after the game.
Time didn't dampen the
enthusiasm.**

The '03 Barons were heroes, and for a time celebrities, in Manheim.

The moments after the game were snow- covered and delirious.

Ten years later,
teamwork and
camaraderie was
what the '03 Barons
remembered most.

Chapter 11:
Where are they now?

A few days after the game, Wilt was sitting in Chad's Barbershop, an old-school hangout on the town square in Manheim, waiting to get a haircut. The topic of conversation was … well, you can imagine. One man got a haircut, paid and left. Then he did a double-take and came back inside. "Wait … you're Shawn Wilt?" Wilt wouldn't be paying for his haircut. A few days later, he was standing in line at A&M Pizza when somebody recognized him again. Free hoagie. It was another few years before Wilt could legally drink at local taprooms,

but when he did, the free beers started coming.

In the game's giddy aftermath, there were state championship T-shirts, sweatshirts, hats, bumper stickers, Christmas ornaments, posters, refrigerator magnets, lapel pins, DVDs, videotapes, jackets, model trucks, football-helmet air fresheners and, most appropriate of all, snow globes. The football booster club grossed about $100,000 in state championship apparel alone, with all profits going back into the football program. At least 200 snow globes were sold, most at $45 and some, autographed by Williams, at $60. (The extra 15 bucks per globe went to the Manheim Recreation Commission.) About 500 model trucks sold at $60 apiece. The community raised about $20,000 to buy the players and coaches gaudy, Super Bowl-style rings, which cost $260 each.

All of the 2003 Barons were heroes and, within town limits, celebrities. But most of them, the seniors at least, quickly moved on. Mike Byrne and Jarryd Moyer accepted scholarship offers to Delaware, then a national power in Division 1-AA college football. Byrne had an excellent four-year career there as an offensive lineman, then went to the Miami Dolphins' training camp as an undrafted free agent. He stuck there for a while, but was eventually released and caught on with the Calgary Stampeders of the Canadian Football League, where he was part of a Grey Cup championship in 2008. Byrne played at various levels of Arena Football as recently as 2012. He has settled in Baltimore, where he sells medical equipment and follows the Ravens, quarterbacked by Byrne's buddy and college teammate Joe Flacco.

Moyer played two years at Delaware. Flacco arrived there, as a transfer from Pitt, in the spring of Moyer's second year. "With that guy being there, I knew I had to do everything if I was going to play," he said. Moyer now believes he overdid the weight room. A bad back dating to his high school days became a herniated disc, and his playing days were over. He graduated from Delaware and now works as a regional manager for Power Train, a chain of gyms owned by Steve Saunders, an L-L League alumnus who's become a sought-after trainer for pro athletes. Byrne has also worked for Saunders and trained at Power Train. So has Conti, the Pine-Richland lineman, and Walker, now the Pittsburgh Pirates' everyday second baseman. Conti played college football at Bucknell, and then played professionally in Europe. Although he's now a financial adviser in Pittsburgh, he has dual citizenship in Italy and is a member of something most Americans would be surprised to know exists: the Italian national football team. Moyer recalls being at Power Train's Manheim gym and overhearing Walker, there to work out, talking about an amazing high school football game he had played in. Talking, in fact, about this quarterback the other team had, who was deceptively fast and tough. Moyer sidled up. "Are you talking about me?" he asked.

Neil Hershey moved on to the University of Virginia, where he got a chemistry degree. He's now at the University of Michigan, completing a doctorate in chemistry. He will soon argue his thesis, a timeless classic: "Measuring Molecules in Rat Brains by Microdialysis." Kevin Hershey, Neil's twin, was also scholarly. He attended the University of Pittsburgh and Pitt's law school, and is now a patent attorney. Rob Trovato, the self-proclaimed "stupidest guy" on the line, graduated from Millersville University with a teaching certification. Unable to find a teaching job, he trained to become a firefighter, which he now does for a living in Montgomery County, Md., commuting from his Lancaster County home a couple times a week to work 24-hour shifts. For a while, after the season, Trovato also became the biggest guy on the line, crossing the 300-pound mark. Then he made some lifestyle changes, and his weight fell as low as 200. Recently, he said, he got back into serious lifting and weighs about 240.

Plowman is also a Pitt grad, now enlisted in the U.S. Army and completing physician's assistant training in Roanoke, Va. Krause played football at Lebanon Valley College. He teaches technical education at Warwick Middle School and remains on Williams' staff as the outside linebackers coach and head JV coach. Eric Meyers stayed in the area. He works in the home-remodeling business and has settled comfortably into the roles of husband and father.

Hunter rushed for 1,000 yards and 19 touchdowns as a junior in 2004, and made first-team all-state as a linebacker. By the end of that season, he had 30 scholarship offers, including ones from Ohio State and Michigan. But it wasn't all good. In October 2004, Williams and the team went to an Elizabethtown multiplex to watch "Friday Night Lights," the film version of Buzz Bissinger's book about high school football fanaticism in Texas. The film included a wild booze party leading to teen sex, a parent coming on the practice field to berate and then physically assault his son for fumbling, a coach coming home after a loss to find a dozen "For Sale" signs on his front lawn, and the coach telling his players, "You have the responsibility of protecting this team and this school and this town."

"Manheim is exactly the same," Jeremiha Hunter said afterward. "Just smaller." Hunter probably didn't mean that as literally as it sounded. Still, Williams acknowledged that the 2003 season was sort of a honeymoon period for Hunter and his family in Manheim. The kid was a sophomore trying to fit in with a strong senior class. The Hunters never got comfortable in Manheim, according to Williams. "I know that many of our parents tried to get them involved," Williams said. "I told (Brian) that people here will let you in, if you let them. They weren't interested." Brian Hunter acknowledged as much. "Mike is right about that; I'm glad he said it," Hunter said. "Our business was in York, and we're not party people."

But Hunter, who is African-American, also said the difference between the 2003 and 2004 seasons was like night and day. He recalled being on the field while the team was warming up before a game against Solanco in September 2004, when he noticed his son wasn't there. He went inside the locker room and found Jeremiha lying on the floor in the shower room in his underwear. Jeremiha said he had heard the N-word from some Solanco people. "I practically had to dress him and get him on the field," Hunter said. Later that year, Brian came home to find his son in tears. "You hit Jeremiha with a baseball bat, and he won't cry," Hunter said. "We kind of had a family meeting. I had to get to the bottom of what was going on. Jeremiha said he's totally unhappy. I wasn't going to let people run us out of town, but then (Xzavier) said something. He said, 'I thought you always told us high school was supposed to be fun. We're not having fun.' That broke my heart."

Williams said Jeremiha had stopped working hard, a charge Brian Hunter vehemently denied. Brian Hunter says his family dealt with racism that increased and became overt in 2004, a charge Williams finds dubious. By spring, there were rumors that the Hunters were leaving Manheim. "I have a lot of thoughts," Williams told the Intell, "but not a lot of answers." Hunter eventually announced that his family was indeed moving to Harrisburg, and Jeremiha was transferring to the science and technology magnet school attached to Harrisburg High School, where he'd play for George Chaump, the John Harris coach from the old Central Penn League. "I have the utmost respect for Mike Williams as a football man," Brian Hunter said. "I really think we're more alike than we are different. I have a lot of love for that 2003 team, but in 2004, things happened, and it left a bad taste."

"How (the Hunters) got here and how (they) left is not a great story for high school football," Williams said. "Maybe we did compromise our principles. Does it look bad? I would kind of agree that it does." Brian Hunter has gone on to coach as an assistant at several high schools in Pennsylvania and Arizona, currently at Dover High in York County. Jeremiha went to the University of Iowa, where he

> *"How (the Hunters) got here and how (they) left is not a great story for high school football."*
> **Mike Williams**

started at linebacker for three years, led the
Hawkeyes in tackles as a senior, and was named
second team All-Big Ten. He was signed by the
New Orleans Saints as an undrafted free agent
in late July 2011. A week later, he tore an Achil-
les tendon and spent the 2011 season on injured
reserve. The Saints waived him in April 2012.
He got an offer to join the Toronto Argonauts
of the CFL, but turned it down, thinking he had
not fully recovered from his injury. He has not

> *"I wasn't necessarily a military guy growing up. Working at a bar in Fort Lauderdale was a blast, but the military pre-sented itself, gave me a chance to get training I wanted."*
>
> Shawn Wilt

played football since, but hasn't given up on the game. He is now thoroughly
rehabbed, according to Brian Hunter. He met with Arizona Cardinals coach
Bruce Arians just before training camp, but hasn't received an offer. As this was
written, Hunter was still waiting for the phone to ring.

Shawn Wilt played for two years at Division II Shippensburg University, then transferred to Florida Atlantic University in Boca Raton to major in
mechanical engineering. Florida Atlantic played Division I football and was
coached by former Miami coach Howard Schnellenberger. Wilt wanted to walk
on there, but his new major wouldn't allow it. While at Florida Atlantic, he was
part of a team that built a Formula One race car, and another that won an in-
ternational competition to build and race a self-propelled sub. He was the sub
driver because he had the strongest legs for pedaling. Wilt also joined a Navy
program that paid for his education — he'd been working at a bar to that point
— and would provide training as a submarine officer upon graduation. He's
now stationed in San Diego, where he's an engineering officer supervising the
nuclear reactor on the USS Jefferson City, a submarine which had been at sea for
seven weeks when he took time for an interview in June 2013. "I wasn't necessarily a military guy growing up," he said. "Working at a bar in Fort Lauderdale
was a blast, but the military presented itself, gave me a chance to get training I
wanted. And I guess I started thinking about what's going on in the world, and
in our lives, what's really important." He said he'll eventually learn to drive the
sub.

Defensive end Ryan Buchter was one of the guys making snow angels that
night in Hershey. He enlisted in the Marines and was sent to Iraq in 2005. His
unit was on a sweep through the town of Husaybah, looking for insurgents in
homes, when Buchter kicked open a door and found what he was looking for.
An insurgent — perhaps an al-Qaida operative, perhaps not — was lying inside
the house. He turned toward Buchter, pulled the pin on a hand grenade and
lobbed it at him. The grenade went off. There was horrific noise, then pain, then
blood. Buchter sustained trauma to his right hand and left leg, which at one

point swelled to four times its normal size. Shrapnel hit him in the face. Protective eyeware probably saved his sight. Somehow, he was alive.

Buchter got out of the house and onto a stretcher, which was loaded onto a tank that took him to a medical unit. Doctors did emergency surgery to relieve pressure on the leg. They stitched and stapled him together. They marveled that their patient wasn't in far worse shape. "The doctors couldn't figure out how I didn't lose my leg, or how I didn't die," Buchter told the Lancaster New Era's Jeff Reinhart for a story in the Nov. 29, 2005, edition. He retired from the Marines with a Purple Heart and returned home to get a degree in kinesiology from West Chester University. He's married, with a son born in the summer of 2013. As of August, Buchter was working at Lebs Mobile Wash, the same business he worked for in high school.

Fresh from Iraq in November 2005, Buchter gave the Barons an emotional pregame talk before their 42-14 defeat of Northern York in the district semifinals. "That was probably the coolest thing I've ever seen before a football game," Graham Zug, a senior wideout who later played at Penn State, told Reinhart. Buchter says he's fully functional physically — itself a small miracle — but the transition to civilian life hasn't been easy. "It was a challenge at first," he said. "I've gotten a lot of support from the community."

Central football is still a big deal, of course. The Barons were supposed to be rebuilding in 2004, but went 13-2 and got to the state final again thanks to a riveting 16-13 defeat of, yes, Berwick in the state semifinal. At the time, Williams said the win was as big as, or bigger than, Pine-Richland in 2003. "For me, personally, it is," he said. "I've taken a lot of razzing. I've gotten letters from people saying we can't beat Berwick." The triumph was leavened considerably by a 56-20 loss to Thomas Jefferson in the final.

Central has been very good, but not quite dominant, since. It won district titles in 2005 and 2009. The '09 team was led by all-state end Dakota Royer, who got a scholarship to Penn State. The team went all the way to the state final, where it lost a 10-7 battle to Selinsgrove. Williams sees that as one that got away. "We should have won that state title," he said. "We could have won a couple of them."

But things had changed. It was getting harder for Central to out-X-and-O people. Selinsgrove coach Dave Hess, an assistant when Central was lighting up the coal region from 1999 to 2003, admitted that playing the Barons then helped his program move into the 21st century. Section Two of the L-L was getting better, especially with the emergence of Lampeter-Strasburg under a terrific young coach, John Manion. The Pioneers beat Central in districts in 2010. Also, Bishop McDevitt, a Harrisburg-area talent farm that produced NFL stars Ricky Watters

Watters and LeSean McCoy, moved down a class to AAA and entered the 2013 season with a streak of three straight district titles.

Williams is 68. His record of 327-70-3 is, by light-years, the best in L-L history and the best among active coaches in District Three. He has long since retired as a teacher, but is not seriously considering it as a coach. His finest moment as a coach came from his saddest one. On Jan. 16, 2011, after a team brunch in Manheim, four Central players — freshman DeVaughn Lee, sophomores Nicolas Bryson and Cody Hollinger, and junior John Griffith — were killed in an auto accident. It was an unimaginable gut-punch to a team, a school and a community. Williams was asked to speak at a memorial service for the players Friday, Jan. 21, at LCBC Church in Manheim.

He wrote down some things he wanted to say. When he tried to say them for an audience of only his wife, Linda, he couldn't do it. He couldn't even begin. He went to the auditorium early that night, went off by himself in a back room and "tried to get my game face on." He couldn't do it then, either. The service began. More than a thousand people packed the place. Everyone was dressed for church except for the Central players, who sat in game jerseys, their heads bowed in what could have been prayer or anguish. Williams was himself dressed for a game, in Baron maroon Under Armour. They called his name.

> "*If there's a football team in heaven, they're on it. And excuse me for saying so, but they're kicking ass.*"
> Mike Williams

"All of a sudden I was totally calm," he said. He talked about that awful Sunday and the healing that will come, indeed that had already begun. He talked about something football coaches don't often discuss: love. "We put up a front," he said. "We talk tough. We act tough. There's no other way to do it." He said coaches sometimes remind players that they love them, but quickly add, "We love you more when we win." Laughter, at the perfect time, in the unlikeliest place in the world. He did not even pay lip service to the tiresome observation that in times like these, a game doesn't matter. You mean the game that lit a fire under these boys and sparked their friendship and cemented their bond? Yeah, that game. "If there's a football team in heaven, they're on it," Williams said. "And excuse me for saying so, but they're kicking ass."

"Being Mike Williams, in this town, is kind of a big deal," Kevin Krause said. Never bigger than on that day.

Football coaches and players talk all the time about camaraderie and chemistry and commitment and family. The 2003 team seems to mean it, and still, a decade later, seems to live it. It held a reunion in 2008, the five-year anniversary. Nothing fancy, Byrne said, just "beer and about a zillion wings" at a Manheim eatery. A 10-year reunion was planned for the fall of 2013, but the truth is there are impromptu reunions all the time. Byrne was the best man at Krause's wedding. The Hersheys were groomsmen for Trovato. Most of the seniors got together as recently as July 2013, for Moyer's wedding in Manheim. And so on. Trovato said when the guys from out of the area come back, there's a pilgrimage to A&M Pizza. It's nostalgic. "You run into any of those guys at the mall, or wherever," Buchter said, "and you pick right back up."

Krause has been around a lot of football teams now, as a player and a coach. "I can't say I've been around a group as tight as that one is," he said. "Not even close."

Aug. 29	Central Dauphin	30-3
Sept. 5	at Middletown	35-0
Sept. 12	Hempfield	55-6
Sept. 19	at Lebanon	49-7
Sept. 26	at Warwick	35-0
Oct. 3	Garden Spot	45-6
Oct. 10	at Elizabethtown	38-0
Oct. 17	Ephrata	28-19
Oct. 25	at Conestoga Valley	28-0
Oct. 31	Solanco	61-0
TOTAL		**404-41**

Archives I:

The Regular Season

Aug. 30:

Barons Ty one on Rams

McCauley's three TDs help Central avenge loss to CD, 30-3

By Kevin Freeman
Intelligencer Journal

Last year, it was Central Dauphin with all the experience.

This year, it was Manheim Central's turn to turn the tables.

Tyler McCauley scored three touchdowns as the Barons avenged last season's 51-22 loss to the Rams with a 30-3 victory on a steamy Friday night at Manheim's Eldon Rettew Field.

Manheim's seasoned offensive and defensive lines along with poised quarterback Jarryd Moyer enabled the Barons to take an early lead. Their stingy defense allowed them to keep it.

McCauley crossed the goal line three times but there were many stars for the Barons, not the least of which

was Moyer, who rushed for a game-high 81 yards on nine carries and threw for 177 yards and a TD on 7-for-14 passing.

Sure, the Barons were looking for revenge after last year's loss. But on the whole, this was two different teams than faced one another last year.

"It's still a sweet victory," Moyer said.

The game was only three minutes old when the Barons took a 7-0 lead. The six-play, 83-yard drive, culminating with McCauley's first TD (a two-yard run) was highlighted by Moyer's 51-yard scamper down the left sideline.

It was a play Manheim's quarterbacks have run forever, many times with success. Moyer sticks the ball in

Craig Gatchell takes on a Hempfield defender.

a running back's stomach, removes it and takes off.

Moyer's 18-yard pass to Tyler Swarr got the ball inside the Rams' 10 and was also a key to the drive.

Central Dauphin, a shadow of the team that won the District Three Class AAAA title last season (three returning starters), was able to move the ball with quarterback Kevin Rombach (19-for-32, 172 yards) at the controls. Three-and-outs were rare but CD, which had eight different players catch a pass, never got close to scoring in the first half.

"We feared their big guys would make plays off the screen pass but we did a good job defensing that," said Manheim Central coach Mike Williams.

Manheim newcomer Jeremiha

Hunter had a lot to do with halting CD's drives. He forced a fumble midway through the first quarter and got a hand on a lateral pass that was scooped up by Ryan Dennes and returned to the CD 10.

Ryan Huber turned that turnover into three points — and a 10-0 Barons' lead — with a 36-yard field goal.

First-year CD coach Paul Plott questioned the turnover. He thought the pass was going forward when Hunter deflected it. But the ruling went the Barons' way.

Central took a 17-0 lead with three minutes left in the half. The Barons went 74 yards in only three plays, thanks to Moyer's slant pass and run-after-catch by Shawn Wilt that went for 65 yards. CD's Steve Cooper prevented Wilt from scoring with a string tackle at the Rams' 10. But Mc-Cauley (nine carries, 32 yards) finished the job with a four-yard rumble off right tackle.

Manheim right guard Kevin Hershey and right tackle Rob Trovato cleared out the left side of CD's line for McCauley.

"They (the offensive line) were just blowing those guys off," McCauley said. "I had a lot of room to run."

The Barons may have been content to run out the clock when they got the ball at midfield with 15.7 seconds left in the first half.

But Eric Meyers (six-47) broke off a 25-yard run, breaking tackles and dragging tacklers. After an incomplete pass, the Barons had the ball on the CD 34 with :02.5 left.

Five Barons wideouts trotted onto the field and everybody knew the next pass was going to the end zone, which is just what happened. Moyer found Wilt in the end zone down the right side. Moyer made the play when he deftly sidestepped the pass rush before delivering the ball.

"That was a big time move," Williams said.

With a 23-0 lead at halftime, the Barons' offense couldn't get much going in the third quarter. Neither team did, really, with both battling the draining humidity-induced heat.

Central Dauphin saw a drive die with three straight incompletions at the Manheim 17 and opted for a field goal, which Tony Bernatos hit from 33 yards out. It was their only score of the game.

"We're very young, mostly sopho-mores and juniors," Plott said. "We have no game-experience and that hurt us. We made too many mistakes."

The Barons tacked on a TD in the dying moments of the game. They got the ball at midfield after a failed CD onsides kick and drove to the Rams' 1 where McCauley — and the O-line — did what they do best.

Like most coaches, Williams tends to see the warts before he sees the positives. Sure, the Barons substitu-tions were at times rocky. And there were eight penalties for 50 yards.

But Central started the season with a win, a win over a Class AAAA school.

"CD plays in one of the top leagues in the state," Williams said. "Any-time you can beat someone from that league, it's a great win."

Sept. 6:

Middletown no match for Central

Moyer throws for 242 yards as versatile Barons wallop Blue Raiders, 35-0

By Ed Gruver
Intelligencer Journal

MIDDLETOWN — Manheim Central senior Mike Byrne bore no visible signs of physical combat Friday night, no bruises or scratches were in evidence as he appeared in the Barons' locker room clad in a towel.

Central had mauled Middletown 35-0 at War Memorial Field, had man-handled the Blue Raiders both offensively and defensively. Byrne, one of the Barons' team captains and a two-way lineman, was one of those who played a significant role as Central relied on force to deal with Middletown's finesse.

"Eventually we got rolling," Byrne said. "And once we get rolling, we're hard to stop."

The Barons, now 2-0 in the non-league season, needed a little time to adjust to the Blue Raiders' schemes. Middletown opened the game defensively with a nine-man front, a new look for them that coordinator Rich Bisking drew up this week.

Offensively, the Raiders (1-1) relied in a Wing-T set traditional to Mid-Penn Conference teams, hoping their intricate counters and traps could slow Central's pursuit.

"They played finesse," Byrne said, "but we try to play finesse and hard. And I think our hard game won out.

"We always try to outdo the other team, get 'em on their heels and wear 'em down in the second half. We're in pretty good condition, so we'll just keep going."

Central didn't take long to get going Friday. Defensive tackle Neil Hershey's recovery of a Middletown fumble -- one of four turnovers the Blue Raiders endured in the game -- set up the Barons' first touchdown, a 20-yard strike from QB Jarryd Moyer to wide receiver Tyler Swarr with 13 seconds left in the opening quarter.

Moyer (10-21-242-1) made it 13-0 when he found wideout Ryan Dennes on an 11-yard slant over the middle 5:33 before the half.

The Barons' recovery of another Blue Raiders' fumble led to a 19-0 lead, Dennes making an acrobatic one-handed grab of a Moyer pass in the end zone with 2:37 to go in the second quarter.

Central's fast start was enough to impress Middletown coach Mike Donghia. "I think they're stronger (than last year)," he opined.

"We should be (stronger than a year ago)," Barons boss Mike Williams said. "We have some guys who are pretty studly up front, pretty strong."

The Barons increased their lead quickly in the second half, scoring the first two times they had the ball. Moyer's third TD pass of the game, a slant over the middle to end Ryan Huber from 35 yards out, made it 25-0 midway through the third.

"He's a class kid," Donghia said of Moyer. "Supercomposure. When something goes wrong, he gets up and shakes it off. You can't say enough about that kind of leadership."

Defensive back Shawn Wilt followed with an interception of a Jon Bailes pass six seconds later, and running back Jeremiha Hunter increased Central's lead to 35-0 when he followed right guard Kevin Hershey to the end zone from 21 yards out.

Eli Esh closed the scoring with a 35-yard field goal with 3:38 left in the game.

Middletown was minus its starting backfield of halfback Ren Rosario and fullback Darby Hughes, but Donghia refused to use that as an excuse and focused instead on turnovers.

"We need a little more mental toughness in order to avoid those kinds of mistakes," he said. "Especially against a great football team."

Sept. 13:

Barons bludgeon Knights

End series, for now, with 55-6 victory

By Ed Gruver
Intelligencer Journal

Upset at what they deemed an unceremonious departure from Hempfield's football schedule next season, Manheim Central wanted to leave a lasting impression on its longtime rival.

The Barons accomplished just that, scoring touchdowns on seven of their first nine possessions en route to a 55-6 non-league win Friday night at rainslick Elden Rettew Field.

The victory was one of the most lopsided in the history of a county rivalry that dates back five decades. Central leads the series 16-9-1, but the Black Knights were coming off a 26-10 win last season in Hempfield.

"We knew it was probably the last time we're going to play them for a long time, and we wanted to go out with the win," said senior QB Jarryd Moyer, who rushed for three touch-

From a fight in the mud with Ephrata: Jarryd Moyer tries to fight past the Mounts' Nick Ream.

downs and threw for one.

"Coach (Mike Williams) got us pumped up and we came ready to play."

Williams said he spoke to his team before the game about the history of the rivalry, which began in 1960 when Williams was a Barons' sophomore. Black Knights boss Tom Getz has also figured in the series as both a coach and player, graduating from Central in 1967 after winning a lineman award for his outstanding play at center.

"It was somewhat (of a motivational factor)," Williams said of Hempfield's decision to drop the Class AAA Barons from their schedule in favor of adding a Class AAAA opponent.

"We talked about it but didn't overemphasize it because it was more of an adult thing. Tom and I are good friends, and how it came about was not as, how we say, good as it should've been. We should've had a little more discussion as to how it came about.

"Anybody can drop us (from their schedule), it's just a question of how you do it."

Sufficiently motivated, Central (3-0) carried a 20-6 lead into halftime, then broke the game open with three touchdowns in the third quarter.

"They're a good football team, no doubt about it," Getz said. "They did whatever they wanted to on offense, and we couldn't stop them."

Fronted by an offensive line featuring center Mike Byrne, guards Ty Leese and Neil Hershey and tackles Kevin Hershey and Rob Trovato, Baron backs rushed for 419 yards and averaged nearly 10 yards per carry.

"Our line did an excellent, excellent job tonight," said Moyer, who gained 72 yards on seven carries. "Give all the credit to them. Every play it seemed like we were getting 10 yards a clip."

Moyer started the scoring, going in from the 7 to cap Central's game-opening, 11-play, 54-yard march.

The Knights (2-1) responded with a 10-play, 78-yard drive, QB Sam Shuman spinning off of several hits to score from the 16.

Central countered with two long scoring drives, Moyer capping the first with an 11-yard TD run and the second with a four-yard scoring toss to wide receiver Ryan Dennes.

The Barons opened the throttle on their offense in the third. Tyler Mc-Cauley, who rushed for a game-high 103 yards on just eight carries, scored on a 52-yard jaunt up the middle to make it 27-6.

Central, which didn't have to punt once the entire evening, followed with TD runs of 10 yards by Moyer and Eric Meyers, a 39-yard run by Craig Gatchell and a 13-yard run by Andy Kirchner.

The 49-point differential seemed stunning to Hempfield, which entered Friday's game looking to make it two wins in a row over the Barons.

"We're not as good as maybe we thought we were," Getz said, "and they're probably better than we expected."

The Knights tried to give Central's defense different looks by alternating QBs Shuman and Austin Hinkle, but the Barons weren't confused. Central surrendered just eight first downs overall.

"We knew when (Shuman) was in, they're running the option, when (Hinkle) is in, they're going to throw more," Williams said. "It took us a little while, but we adjusted."

Sept. 20:

Hunter, Central storm past Cedars, 48-7

By Joel Schreiner
Intelligencer Journal

LEBANON — The folks in Lebanon thought they had seen the last of the tropical weather. That is, until another system blew through Saturday night.

Hurricane Baron, packed with strong arms and a powerful defense, swept through Lebanon Stadium, leaving behind a path of destruction that left many gazing in disbelief.

Leading by a touchdown at halftime, Manheim Central racked up 35 unanswered points, including 28 in the fourth quarter, en route to a 47-7 thrashing of the Cedars in the Hurricane Isabel-delayed Section Two opener for both teams.

"In the second half we just came out fired up," said Central quarterback Jarryd Moyer. "We were really flat in the first half and I have no idea why."

Head Baron Mike Williams has an idea.

"I think we were a little too big for our britches to be truthful," Williams declared.

Central (1-0 Section Two, 4-0 overall) did enter the game on a 12-game winning streak over Lebanon, dating back to 1991. In fact, Lebanon has never conquered the Barons.

Leading 14-7 at the break, Central forced the Cedars to punt on their first possession of the second half. The Baron offensive attack then quickly dealt a crushing blow to Lebanon (0-1, 3-1).

On their first play of the second half, the Barons got a 53-yard touchdown run from Jeremiha Hunter to make it 21-7. For Hunter, it was his second TD of the night. For Central, it was a chance to call a play the coaches talked about at halftime.

"We saw they were blitzing a lot on first down and really packing it in, so we wanted to take it outside," explained Williams. "That play really helped us."

Moyer agreed.

"I think that really took all the wind out of them," Moyer said. "That was such a huge play for us."

From that point on, it was all Central, which has outscored its opponents 169-16 this season.

The Barons went up 28-7 on the first play of the fourth quarter when Moyer hit Ryan Dennes from four yards out. It was the second scoring connection between the two of the night. The first, a 22-yarder, put the Barons ahead for good, 14-7, with 1:38

left in the half.

Little more than a minute later, following a Shawn Wilt interception of Brad Bishop, Central scored again on a 14-yard Moyer run. Three plays later Bishop was picked again, this time deep in his own territory.

Craig Gatchell picked off the shovel pass try and returned it four yards for a TD, giving Manheim a 42-7 lead and invoking the mercy rule.

That's three touchdowns in a span of 2:33 on just three offensive plays.

Bishop was 8-of-19 on the night and was picked off three times, all in the decisive second half.

"We knew what we had to do in the second half," said Baron lineman Mike Byrne. "I'm not sure what happened, but something clicked at halftime."

Central's second-team offense closed out the scoring wth a three-yard run from Gatchell with 2:16 left.

"We made some big plays on defense," Williams said. "I didn't think we could wear them out, but ultimately I think we did."

Sept. 27

Barons hogtie Warriors

Central's defense limits Warwick to 78 yards

By Joel Schreiner
Intelligencer Journal

Mike Williams will be the first to admit that it's rare for any sophomore to play both ways in his Manheim Central football program.

This must be a rare year then. So rare, in fact, that Williams has not one, but two sophs lining up on both sides of the ball.

One of them, Jeremiha Hunter, is doing so because he is that good and Williams knows it. The other, Nate Mast, has been playing defense but had to join the Baron backfield this week due to an injury.

Thanks in large part to both, the Barons literally ran past Warwick, 35-0, in a Section Two game Friday night at Grosh Field in Lititz. Central is now 2-0 in the section and 5-0 overall.

Hunter and Mast were part of a rushing attack that churned out 336 yards, including 174 in the second half when the Barons went exclusively to the ground game, never throwing a pass.

"We weren't getting guys open so we decided to stick with the run," said Jarryd Moyer, the league's highest-rated quarterback who rushed for a game-high 131 yards on 17 carries.

"We really didn't need to (pass), but we would have liked to a little bit more."

Moyer was an efficient 5-of-8 through the air for 61 yards and a TD, a 29-yarder to Ryan Dennes that gave Central a 14-0 with 8:44 left in the second quarter.

Hunter and Mast, both linebackers, are also part of the ferocious Baron defense that held the Warrior offense to zero total yards in the second half en route to its second shutout of the season.

Warwick (0-2, 2-3) had its chances in the first half, but came up empty. Quarterback Austin Heacock was picked off in the end zone on a third-and-8 from the Baron 14 on the Warriors' opening drive.

On their next drive, they had an 83-yard TD pass from Heacock to Chris Ciccarone called back because Heacock was over the line of scrimmage when he threw the ball.

"We played well in the first half, but we have a bad habit right now of shooting ourselves in the foot," said Warwick coach Bob Locker. "We're making mistakes we shouldn't be making. It's not a lack of effort, it's a lack of execution."

Leading 14-0 at halftime, Mast energized the Baron defense by being part of back-to-back sacks of Heacock on the Warriors' opening drive of the third quarter.

Following a Warwick punt, Hunter capped a seven-play, 57-yard drive

with a five-yard touchdown run to give the Barons a 21-0 lead with 6:31 left in the third.

"We weren't shaking anyone open on pass routes so we decided we were going to run the ball," explained Williams.

That's where Mast comes in. The 5-foot-9, 175-pounder was in the starting backfield filling in for Tyler McCauley who moved to tight end to replace Kevin Yeagle, who is out indefinitely following an appendectomy earlier this week.

Mast rushed for 66 yards on 10 carries.

"I was excited," Mast said. "Playing varsity football at Manheim, of course I was excited."

Hunter, meanwhile, gained 39 yards on seven carries and scored twice.

The Barons have now scored 70 unanswered points against their opponents going back to last week's 49-7 drubbing of Lebanon and have outscored the opposition 204-16 this season.

"They're really, really good," said Locker.

In Friday's decisive second half, Warwick rushed 15 times for zero yards and Heacock's lone completion was for no gain. Heacock was 5-of-12 for 37 yards and got picked off three times as the Baron defense held Warwick to just 78 total yards.

"The defense is great," said Moyer. "They're all about not giving up touchdowns. They don't want teams to score."

Oct. 4:

Barons lay it on the line again

OL paves way to 45-6 win over Garden Spot

By Kevin Freeman
Intelligencer Journal

How many high school football coaches would sell their souls to have Manheim Central's offensive line?

Dumb question, that. Led by mountain-like Mike Byrne, the 6-foot-5, 265-pound center, there aren't many defensive lines that match the Barons' girth and experience.

While the Barons' beef up front has gotten some recognition, and rightfully so, someone has to actually advance the ball.

That's where the Barons are fortunate, too.

Five different Barons scored touchdowns (one was a defensive TD) en route to a 45-6 defeat of Garden Spot in Manheim Friday night in a battle of Section Two unbeatens. Central (3-0 Section Two, 6-0 overall) built a 38-0 lead at halftime, triggering the mercy rule (continuous clock) in the second half.

While the Barons showed their diversity on offense, they showed ferociousness on defense, limiting the Spartans (2-1, 3-3) to minus 18 yards rushing. As the Barons were building their 38-0 halftime lead, Spot managed only 41 offensive yards.

"They (Manheim) are just better than us up front," said Garden Spot coach Eric Spencer. "That's probably the best front line I've ever seen in my coaching career."

The Barons scored on their first six possessions, needing just five plays and 1:57 to reach the end zone the first time. Jeremiha Hunter (eight carries, 40 yards) scored on an eight-yard run.

The Spartans made their deepest penetration into Manheim territory in the first half on their first drive, advancing to the Central 38. But the drive stalled there on an incomplete pass on fourth down.

From there, the game got one-sided. Eric Meyers (5-45) scored the first of his two TDs on a four-yard run. Hunter made the score 14-0 when he ran in the two-point conversion.

Ryan Huber capped a 10-play drive that saw the Barons convert a fourth-and-eight play with a 43-yard field goal. MC quarterback Jarryd Moyer then hit Ryan Dennes with a 42-yard TD pass and Manheim led 24-0.

Barons defensive lineman Kevin Krause pounced on a fumble at the Garden Spot 9 and on the next play, Moyer kept the ball on the option for a TD and a 31-0 lead.

Central's Nate Mast stepped in front of a Shane Martin pass near the end of the second quarter and returned it 25 yards for a touchdown. "We don't want one guy to get the ball so their defense can concentrate on one guy," said Moyer, who led all rushers with 86 yards and was 6-for-8 for 88 yards passing. "We like to spread it around."

Garden Spot tried to neutralize the Barons' defense with draw plays and screen passes. But having the lead, the Barons could take chances defensively.

"We tried to dink some passes but our kids are young and our quarterback got rattled," Spencer said. "Hey, welcome to the big boys."

Andrew Abreu, Garden Spot's leading rusher who averaged 104.2 yards per game, was limited to 12 yards on 11 carries. Six of his carries went for negative yards. Manheim

Central coach Mike Williams said his defense was keying on stopping Abreu.

"We were scared of him because if you miss him, it's a touchdown," Williams said.

With four games remaining in the regular season, including a penultimate meeting with Conestoga Valley, Section Two's only other undefeated team, the Barons are building as the season progresses. Friday night's win over Garden Spot was another building block.

"Any coach wants to get better each week," Williams said. "There's only one goal (a state title) that can satisfy us. Only one goal that we'll really be happy with. Anything less than that ... would be disappointing. If we're going to compete with the elite teams in Pennsylvania, we just have to keep getting better."

Oct. 11:

Barons overcome errors in 38-0 rout of E-town

Moyer runs for 92 yards, passes for 228 in victory

By Andrew Sheeley
Intelligencer Journal

Manheim Central did a lot of things wrong Friday night in Elizabethtown, but the Barons are so good that it didn't matter.

They gave up 94 penalty yards and four turnovers, but still blew out the host Bears 38-0 in a Lancaster-Lebanon League Section Two tuneup for their showdown with Ephrata next week.

The Barons came out firing, scoring on the third play of the game when senior quarterback Jarryd Moyer broke off a 32-yard run for a touchdown just 1:08 into the game.

After the Bears fumbled away their ensuing possession, the Barons took over at the E-town 35 and five plays later found the end zone again, this time on a 13-yard pass from Moyer to senior wideout Shawn Wilt to make it 14-0 with 6:17 still to play in the first quarter.

From that point on, the Manheim Central offense started to slow down. After Ryan Huber's 39-yard field goal with 3:03 left in the first made it 17-0, the Barons' offense began to make some uncharacteristic mistakes.

E-town's Tim Carpenter intercepted a Moyer pass on the first play of the second quarter, quelling a Manheim drive at the Bears' 17. On the Barons' next possession, Ryan Plowman missed a 24-yard field goal. And on their third chance in the third, Moyer was picked off again, this time by Donald Berkheimer.

"We did some things good and we did some bad things," said Baron coach Mike Williams. "We played well at times, we moved the ball. We had some mental errors."

Despite those mental errors, the Barons took a 24-0 lead when senior running back Eric Meyers ran in from the 2-yard line with 23 seconds remaining in the half.

While the Barons may have struggled offensively, their defense didn't miss a beat. Manheim held the Bears to just six yards rushing on 13 carries in the first half and only 33 yards through the air — a grand total of 39 yards.

The second half was more of the same. After the Bears went four-and-out on their first possession, the Barons took over at their own 17 and promptly marched 83 yards down the field.

Meyers ran it in from five yards out to make it 31-0. Jeremiha Hunter's eight yard touchdown with 9:56 left to play rounded out the scoring at 38-0.

"E-town played hard," said Williams. "But I thought we dominated the game. You get these situations when you're not focused and you get those miscues. We still had 38 points, but we could have had. ... Hopefully this was a good game for us to get those mistakes out of our system."

For the game, Moyer racked up 92 yards rushing on eight carries and threw for 228 yards on 15-of-22 passing. Wilt caught five balls for 96 yards and also intercepted a pass, while sophomore running back Nate Mast contributed 64 yards on 10 carries.

For the Bears, offense was sparse as they could only muster 145 total yards. Carpenter caught four passes for 57 yards. The Barons forced the Bears to turn the ball over five times in the game.

Now the Barons have to hope their problems don't carry over to next week's game against the Mountaineers.

"I'm not worried about that," said Williams. "Every team over the course of the season has a down week. We had a sloppy practice this week. It's amazing with teenagers how well they play when the money's on the line. We'll be more intense next week."

Oct. 18:

Central's focus is rewarding

Survive Ephrata, 29-18, eye game against CV

By Ed Gruver
Intelligencer Journal

On a rain-slick night when Manheim Central lost starting safety Shawn Wilt to a season-ending leg injury, the Barons almost lost their grip on a section title and district playoff berth.

Instead, Manheim Central lineman Neil Hershey watched teammate Jeremiha Hunter gallop 37 yards through the mud on an interception return for a touchdown, and knew the late score did more than just seal a 29-18 Section Two win over Ephrata Friday night at Elden Rettew Field.

It allowed the unbeaten Barons, 5-0 in the section and 8-0 overall, to turn their thoughts to next Saturday's Section Two showdown at Conestoga Valley. The Buckskins (4-1, 7-1) beat Elizabethtown 46-0 Friday behind QB Jordan Steffy's six TD passes.

"CV's a great team," said Hershey, a senior letterman and team captain who recovered a fourth-quarter fumble and helped open holes for a Baron ground game that produced two 100-yard rushers and totaled 341 yards of terra firma.

"We'll have to play our best game," Hershey added, "so we'll be in the weight room (this) morning thinking about CV."

For most of Friday night's mud-caked Homecoming game with Ephrata (3-2, 5-3), it was all the Barons could do to stop thinking about the Bucks in another fashion — CV's overtime loss at Lebanon last week.

"I talked about it all week long, and that it could happen if we're not ready to play," Central coach Mike Williams said. "Ephrata's a good team and we were ready to play. We just didn't play that well.

"When it was (22-18) and we just gave them the ball again (on a turnover), I was thinking, 'Well, they'll be laughing over at CV this weekend.'"

Central's win was forged despite the loss of Wilt, a senior who was tied for the team lead in interceptions with four and ranked second in tackles with 63. Wilt was injured late in the first quarter when he attempted to make a tackle on Dubbs' 17-yard completion to wide receiver Ryan Bramble (seven receptions for 125 yards, 2 TDs) near the Ephrata sideline. Wilt stayed down for several minutes before his right leg was placed in an inflatable cast and he was taken from the field in an ambulance.

Hunter's touchdown, his third of the game, came courtesy of a Baron blitz that forced Mountaineers QB Derek Dubbs (10-20-154, 2 int.) to hurry his throw. Hunter stepped in front of the short pass at the Ephrata 37 and navigated a slippery trek to the end zone.

Dubbs' pass appeared to wobble, and when Ken Grove was asked if his quarterback was having difficulty gripping the ball in the wet weather, the Ephrata coach nodded.

"We went through the eight or nine balls that we use (during a game)," Grove said. "It was muddy. What happens is that the ball sits in the mud (between plays) and then it's snapped to him."

A steady rain turned the field into a slick quagmire, and turned the game into a battle of turnovers. The two teams combined to turn the ball over 10 times, five times each. In the fourth quarter alone there were a combined six turnovers, but only Hunter's interception resulted in a score.

Neither team had problems with the weather early on. In a game that matched Central's league-leading offense against an Ephrata defense that ranks fourth in the L-L, it was the Barons who took control at the outset.

Hunter, who rushed for 141 yards on 22 carries, capped a 12-play, 79-yard game-opening drive when he slanted into the end zone behind right guard Kevin Hershey.

Matt Burkholder's 82-yard kickoff return set the tone for a night in which the Mounts consistently enjoyed good field position. From the Barons' 15-yard line, Ephrata needed five plays before Dubbs found Bramble in the end zone on a four-yard scoring pass.

Ephrata's two-point conversion failed, and the Barons built their lead to 14-6 by driving 80 yards in six plays late in the half. Eric Meyers (20-110) ran it in from the 21 behind center Mike Byrne, but the Mounts again responded to a long Baron drive by making a big play of their own.

Ephrata senior back Nate Rock, who ranks fifth among L-L rushers, skirted left tackle and raced 72 yards down the sideline for a score.

The Barons nudged their lead to 20-12 on their opening series of the

Ryan Dennes was one of a battalion of skill-positioned players Hempfield, and most opponents, couldn't stop.

second half. Hunter scored his second TD of the game, a two-yard drive up the middle, but Ephrata countered with another quick strike — a 70-yard TD pass from Dubbs to Bramble.

Barons punter Jeremy Smith pinned the Mounts deep in their territory when his kick rolled out of bounds at the 7 with 14 seconds to go. On first down, Central's defense stacked Rock up at the line of scrimmage, then pushed him back into the end zone for a safety. Believing Rock's forward progress had been stopped, Grove disputed the play later.

More opportunities awaited the Mounts. Ephrata forced and recovered two Baron fumbles in the fourth quar-

ter, but the Mounts turned it over four times — once at Central's 2-yard line and another time on Hunter's pickoff. Barons defensive back Tyler Swarr helped keep the Mounts at bay with two fourth-quarter fumble recoveries.

"We had our chances," Grove said. "Our kids showed a lot of heart, a lot of effort."

Across the muddy field, Williams was a little less enthusiastic about his team's performance.

"It's not one of those games where you went out and dominated and feel good about the way you played," he said. "It's one of those games where you feel you're lucky to have hung on to win."

Oct. 26:

Central smells blood, then draws it

By Mike Gross
Sunday News

For two tense, violent quarters, Manheim Central and Conestoga Valley stared each other down like two Samurais, swords drawn, each unwilling to make the first move.

Then CV blinked. The Barons smelled the kill and did what they usually do.

With a devastating third-quarter blitz, Central beat its archrival for the 16th straight time, 28-0 before an overflow crowd at CV Saturday night.

It means the Barons improve to 9-0, clinch the Lancaster-Lebanon League Section II championship and, barring a miraculous series of events, clinch the top seed for the upcoming District Three Class AAA playoffs.

It also means they burnish their legend. Central was in some trouble through much of the first half, outplayed and beaten on the line of scrimmage.

CV (7-2, 4-2 in the section) was playing for a piece of the section title and to keep faint Class AAAA district hopes alive against the team it wants to beat most, regardless of the stakes.

"No question, they beat us up front," Central coach Mike Williams admitted. "They put it to us on the line of scrimmage."

The Buckskins had more first downs and yardage before halftime. They possessed the ball long and had much better field position.

But they couldn't score.

Very early, they had deep threat Stephen Smalls behind the Central secondary and quarterback Jordan Steffy barely overthrew him. More importantly, Smalls pulled a hamstring and was done for the night.

Both teams seemed to be playing the first half to get to the second anyway, in terms of playcalling. Now CV was seriously limited.

"He's our vertical threat," CV coach Gerad Novak admitted. "That made it tough to throw down the field."

Still, Steffy, a big, strong, athletic Division One college prospect, was making things happen.

CV rumbled to the Central 19 as the first quarter ended, but on third-and-seven from there Jeremiha Hunter, Central's gifted sophomore linebacker, came up with a huge sack of Steffy.

That meant a 42-yard field goal into strong, steady wind, and even Peter Bennett's powerful leg wasn't enough for that.

As the half was winding down CV blocked a Central punt and took over at the Central 35 with just a second left. Again, dead into the wind.

Rather than throw a Hail Mary

to the end zone, Novak tried Bennett again. This time from 52 yards, and again short.

Novak expected Williams to take the wind in the fourth quarter, but it took it right after halftime.

"We had to have it," Williams said. "They had the momentum."

Just as importantly, Williams appealed to the troops at the half as, evidently, no one else can.

"We didn't scream and holler, but we did appeal to their pride," he said.

Central stuffed the Buckskins on the half's first possession, and a bad snap and bad punt gave Central the ball at the CV 28, going downhill.

Six plays later, all runs, Central QB Jarryd Moyer plunged in from a yard out.

A moment later Central's Ryan Dennes was picking the ball out of the air on a bizarre play in which CV completed a pass, which was then juggled, batted in the air and finally grabbed by Dennes at the CV 14.

Two Eric Meyers runs from there, it was 14-0.

Then came a CV three-and-out, and a punt that the wind devoured. More Meyers, 21-0.

With the third quarter time reading 0:00 on the scoreboard, Williams craftily called time out, knowing the official clock on the field had three seconds left in the quarter.

That meant one more wind-stuffed punt, one more Central drive starting in CV territory and, five plays later, one more Meyers TD.

The four touchdown "drives," covered 38, 14, 35 and 46 yards.

It what seemed like 10 minutes, the game went from a savage defensive struggle Central was losing to 29-zip.

"We were fortunate, to some degree," Williams said. "When they had the field position, we kept them out of the end zone.

"When we had the field position, we were able to take advantage."

Nov. 1:

Barons ready for more

Romp past Solanco, 61-0, in L-L finale

By Kevin Freeman
Intelligencer Journal

When Manheim Central's football team scores a touchdown, the air above the Barons' fans is filled with bubbles.

By the time the Barons had scored their seventh touchdown in the fourth quarter Friday night, the fans had run out of bubbles. Solanco, Manheim Central's guest at Elden Rettew Field, could not contain the Barons' speed and was overwhelmed by its strength in a 61-0 thrashing.

If there is a proper way to head into the district playoffs, Central achieved it, rolling up 435 rushing yards, albeit against a Golden Mules team that had one healthy linebacker out of five that have played the position this season.

The Barons (7-0 Section Two, 10-0 overall), ranked second in the state in Class AAA in the Harrisburg Patriot-News poll, became the 10th Manheim Central team to go 10-0 in the regular season (all since 1980). They have now won 32 straight Section Two games and head into the District Three Class AAA playoffs as the top seed. Central will host No. 4 seed Hershey at 7:30 Friday night in Manheim.

The other Class AAA semifinal pits defending champion Lower Dauphin against West Perry.

"We set out this season to play every game as if it were a playoff game," said Central running back Tyler McCauley. "This was playoff game No. 10 for us."

The Barons, who lost to Lower Dauphin in the last second of a district semifinal last season, will be a better playoff team this season based on at least two things: They have a better defense, particularly in the secondary, and they have Jeremiha Hunter at running back and linebacker.

Hunter rushed for 168 yards on just nine carries and scored three touchdowns to pace the Barons' scoring parade Friday night. The Barons, who also got TDs from Jarryd Moyer (two), Eric Meyers, Mike Byrne and Ben Engle, scored TDs on their first six possessions.

"I think we're ready for the playoffs," said Manheim Central coach Mike Williams. "We played well enough tonight that we know what we have to do and we can do it."

The Barons' defense, which has surrendered only 40 points this season and pitched five shutouts, never let the Golden Mules (1-6, 3-7) past the Manheim 28 in the first half. And defense was without two starters, Shawn Wilt (tibia hairline fracture) and Jeremy Smith (shoulder). Smith may be available next week. Wilt is hoping to be back sometime in the playoffs.

"Jeremiha helps our defense and he had some nice runs (tonight)," Williams said.

Byrne had a good night on defense, too, capping it with the interception of an Adam Blevins shovel pass. Byrne then rumbled 16 yards with the pick for a TD.

Byrne remembers last season's district loss to LD and doesn't want a repeat.

"We don't want it to happen again," he said. "We're highly motivated and we're going to come out more intense."

Meyers said losing like the Barons did last year "would not be fun." He said the defense is more experienced and the communication on the field is better.

"We're talking a lot more," he said.

McCauley agreed with that and added that the communication has brought the team closer.

"We're playing for the person beside us, not for ourselves," he said.

Williams, leading his team into the district playoffs for the 12th straight season, said it's time to focus on the "second" season.

"You try not to talk about the playoffs until you get through the regular season," he said. "Now, we can start talking about the loftier goals. A district championship is the next one. Now the intensity picks up at practice. The pressure is on."

There is pressure because if you lose, you're out.

And in Manheim, that would burst a lot of bubbles.

Archives II:

The Playoffs

Nov. 2:

District football: The usual suspects

*Cumberland Valley, Manheim Central, Delone and Camp Hill
are picked to win titles, advance to state playoffs.*

By Mike Gross
Sunday News

Despite all the complex what-if scenarios you've been reading the past few weeks, the District Three football playoff qualifying system is not as complicated as, say, the BCS, or the Index of Leading Economic Indicators.

It's just that nobody even bothers with comprehensive what-ifs for the BCS or economy, lest they blow out computer mainframes.

Now that the regular season dust has cleared, districts, which begin Friday, have come down mostly to the usual suspects. Cumberland Valley. Manheim Central. Delone. Columbia.

What follows is a class-by-class look at what may happen next. In each class, the field is listed in order of seed.

In this week's first round, seed number one plays four and two plays three, at the higher seed's home field.

DISTRICT THREE PLAYOFFS		
Semifinals		
35	Hershey	13
Finals		
38	Lower Dauphin	0
State playoffs		
50	Shamokin	0

All games will be at 7:30 p.m. Friday.

The Class A and AA finals will be at 7:30 p.m. Friday, Nov. 14, at sites to be determined. The Class AAA and AAAA finals, also at 7:30 p.m., will be at Hersheypark Stadium. The AAA game will be on Friday, Nov. 14, with the AAAA game on Saturday, Nov. 15.

The prediction in each class here is for the championship-game result.

Class AAAA: Seedings: 1. Cumberland Valley (10-0); 2. McCaskey (9-1); 3. Reading (9-1); 4. Harrisburg (8-2).

First round: Harrisburg at Cumberland Valley; Reading at McCaskey.

The breakdown: Cumberland Valley, ranked 23rd nationally by USA Today, is a very well-drilled, straightforward bunch typified by two Penn State recruits: 6-2, 235 fullback Dan Lawlor and 6-6, 318 OL Wyatt Bowman, ...

CV coach Tim Rimpfel is 223-69-3 in 25 seasons, including the 1992 state title. McCaskey returned just one full-time starter from last year, and has had a remarkable year save for a flameout against 2-8 Cedar Crest.

The Red Tornado is superbly coached, and as a program expects to win. McCaskey has speed, toughness and, in Jimmare Jackson, the L-L's highest-rated quarterback.

The Red Tornado reached districts by beating Reading 24-21 Saturday night.

Before Saturday, Reading had been the most dominant team in the area. It had outscored foes 378-46 and invoked the Mercy Rule six times. Closest game was 29-3 over Manheim Township. ...

HB Kalise Cook has scored 10 TDs running, eight receiving, and is averaging 13.7 yards per carry. The school record for single-season TDs is 22, by NFL Hall of Famer Lenny Moore. ...

The other HB, Jason Poulson, averages 19.2 per carry. Poulson, Kalise, QB Nick Galan (rating by NCAA formula: 184) and FB James Bryant form the area's best backfield.

Bryant might be the best all-around football player in the field, regardless of class. He's an all-state linebacker whose brother plays at Pittsburgh. Bryant is being recruited by everyone but, uh, Penn State. Pittsburgh and Miami are said to be the leaders. ...

The Most Valuable Person in the field is probably Harrisburg coach George Chaump, famously paid $87,000 to come over from Central Dauphin and earning his keep, turning a team that went 1-9 a year ago into a power.

Cougars lack only depth, which means look out in the future. Chaump coached arguably the best teams the area has ever produced at John Harris High in the 1960s. ...

For what it's worth, the AAAA field consists of four of the five biggest schools in District Three.

Prediction: Cumberland Valley over Reading in the final. Something like 35-33.

Class AAA: *Seedings:* 1. Manheim

Jeremiha Hunter lit up Hershey for 192 rushing yards.

Central (10-0); 2. Lower Dauphin (9-1); 3. West Perry (8-2); 4. Hershey (8-2).

First round: Hershey at Manheim Central; West Perry at Lower Dauphin.

The breakdown: Manheim Central has dominated L-L Section Two, but also owns blowouts against good AAAA teams Hempfield and Central Dauphin.

The Barons have also mostly dominated this class. Their string of nine straight AAA championships was broken, in dramatic fashion, by Lower Dauphin in last year's semifinals.

After a slight down year last season by its standards, the Barons are back, with size, power, speed, depth, a superb QB in Jarryd Moyer and, of course, coaching. They are a prohibitive favorite. ...

The rest of the field is second-tier Mid-Penn Conference. Lower Dauphin is the defending champ and second seed, but the Falcons were soundly beaten by Hershey Oct. 10. ...

Hershey, 2-8 a year ago, lost to West Perry in week two, a game that decided the third and fourth seeds. ...

West Perry played its best football early, and lost at home to Big Spring Oct. 10.

Prediction: Manheim Central over West Perry in the final.

Class AA: *Seedings:* 1. Wyomissing (10-0); 2. Delone (10-0); 3. Schuylkill Valley (8-2); 4. Littlestown (8-2).

First round: Littlestown at Wyomissing; Schuylkill Valley at Delone.

Breakdown: With 152 wins, Wyomissing's Bob Wolfrum became the winningest coach in Berks County history last week. ...

The Spartans are making their 11th district appearance. They've done it with defense, allowing only 69 points. DB-FB Andy Taylor was all-state on defense last year, and has been offered by Boston College. ...

In a York League showdown Oct. 24, Delone handled Littlestown 21-0, holding the Thunderbolts to six first downs, 77 total yards and a ridiculous minus-27 yards rushing. ...

Schuylkill Valley has almost no football tradition. This is its first eight-win season, and first district appearance. QB Matt Korn has thrown for 12 TDs, run for 10.

Prediction: *Delone over Wyomissing.*

Class A: *Seedings:* 1. Steel-High (9-1); 2. Halifax (9-1); 3. Columbia (8-2); 4. Camp Hill (8-2).

First round: Camp Hill at Steel-High; Columbia at Halifax.

Breakdown: Defending champ Camp Hill started slowly, but is coming fast. The Lions beat Steel-High Oct. 10 and will face the Rollers again in the first round. ...

The Rollers did not play this weekend, having accepted a forfeit from Scotland, which was down to 15 beat-up players. ...

According to the Harrisburg Patriot rankings by the NCAA formula, the midstate's two top passers (Lancaster and Berks County players aren't included) are Camp Hill's Dan Alleman and Steel-High's Ryan Mohn, both in the Mid-Penn Liberty. ...

The Liberty, the small-school division of the Mid-Penn, also has Trinity QB Chris Crane, a Boston College signee. ...

Columbia is in districts for the sixth straight year, eighth time in nine years and 12th time overall. ...

The Crimson Tide, as usual, has an excellent, efficient QB in Ben Marley. They seem to be peaking lately, having outscored their last four opponents 126-7.

The Tide will play Halifax, a small-school postseason fixture in football and basketball in recent years. The Wildcats won the Tri-Valley Conference for the third time in four years. Fourth-year coach Dave Borrell is 38-7.

Prediction: Camp Hill over Columbia.

Nov. 8:

Manheim Steamroller flattens Hershey

Hunter rumbles for 198 yards as Barons win district opener

By Jeffrey Reinhart
Lancaster New Era

Mike Williams has been hesitant to say much about Jeremiha Hunter this season.

After all, Manheim Central's football coach keeps reminding everyone within earshot that the Barons' 6-1, 200-pound halfback/linebacker/hit machine/playmaker is just a sophomore, and he'll get plenty of attention during the next two years.

Sorry, coach, but the future is now. Playing in his first District 3 Triple-A playoff game Friday night in Manheim, Hunter didn't let the spotlight bother him, as he turned in one of the finest performances by a Central sophomore since a paper-thin quarterback named Jeff Smoker led the Barons to the state semifinals in 1997.

Hunter, who transferred to Central from York High last summer, rushed 15 times for a career-high 196 yards —that's an eye-popping 14 yards a carry — and a pair of touchdowns, including a 78-yard romp in the fourth quarter as Central hammered Hershey 35-15 to improve to 26-3 in the District 3 playoffs.

Up next for the Barons (11-0 overall) is a rematch with Lower Dauphin, which knocked Central out in the first round of districts last year with a Hail Mary pass at the horn.

The Triple-A title game is set for Friday at 7:30 p.m. in Hersheypark Stadium, which is Lower Dauphin's home field. The Falcons (10-1) soared past West Perry 31-14 in Friday's other semifinal.

Central can kill two birds with one stone against Lower Dauphin.

The Barons can get a little revenge against the Falcons, who shared the Mid-Penn Capital championship with Hershey this season. And Central can win back the district title it lost last year after the Barons won an incred-

ible 10 consecutive Triple-A championships between 1992-2001.

Central will go for its 13th district title on Friday.

"It's great to be going back to Hershey," Central senior quarterback Jarryd Moyer said. "We're looking forward to playing Lower Dauphin again. It'll be cool to play them again."

Hunter, on the other hand, was scorching hot against Hershey. And his incredible individual effort came on the heels of a dynamite game last Friday, when he rushed for 168 yards and three touchdowns in Central's 61-0 win over Solanco in its Lancaster-Lebanon League Section 2 finale.

Against Hershey (8-3), Hunter picked up right where he left off.

"That sucker ran wild on us," Hershey coach Bob May said. "He's only a sophomore? That's scary."

Scary but true.

That's why Williams has kept his prize pupil under the radar this season. In fact, Hunter, who has rushed for 900 yards and 14 touchdowns and was made a slew of bone-crushing hits from his outside linebacker spot in 11 games, was off-limits to the media until Friday night.

"I just want to play," the soft-spoken star said. "I guess I notice some of the stuff I'm doing. But I have two more years. I guess you could say I'm kind of getting noticed right now. But I know I have my junior year and my senior year ahead of me.

"So right now, everything is the

coach's call."

The coach called Hunter's number early and often Friday night. He scored the lone touchdown of the first half on a 9-yard run that gave the Barons a 7-0 lead with 6:01 to go in the half. That was the score at the break.

Central warmed to the task in the third quarter, scoring three times to build a commanding 35-7 lead. Senior halfback Eric Meyers, who carried 15 times for 103 yards, got the party started with a 20-yard TD run to make it 14-0 with 9:22 to go in the third quarter.

Meyers and Hunter were a lethal 1-2 punch. Moyer was tough to bring down, too. He carried 13 times for 76 yards and had a pair of TDs on the ground as Central piled up 399 yards rushing and 505 yards total, along with 21 first downs. And it wasn't like the Barons did anything fancy. They simply beat up the Trojans in the trenches and kept hammering the ball on the ground.

"The old split-back Veer," Williams said. "It's as old as Noah's Ark, but it came back to haunt them."

They were haunted, mostly, by Meyers and Hunter.

"If they key on me, that opens up room for Eric," Hunter said. "If they key on Eric, that opens up room for me. So you can't key on one of us."

Hershey, which dropped to 0-4 in the district playoffs, including a 61-7 first-round loss to Central two years ago, found that out the hard way.

Moyer had a pair of third-quarter TDs, a 5-yard keeper and a 1-yard dive, the latter making it 28-7 with 2:33 to go as the Barons, behind their mammoth offensive line, took control in the trenches and took the game over for good.

"In the first half, we missed a few blocking assignments," Moyer noted. "But we picked up on those in the third quarter, and we really started to steamroll them."

They got flattened by Hunter, in particular.

Ahead 28-7, Central went for the jugular midway through the fourth quarter when Williams called a "62 trap" and Hunter, lined up next to Moyer in the shotgun, darted through a huge hole up the middle, cut left and sprinted 78 yards for a touchdown.

"I just cut it up," said Hunter, whose dad, Brian, is an assistant coach under Williams. "(Junior offensive guard) Ty Leese made a great block and I just took off. The line was opening up some huge holes. Our line is strong and quick, and they can open up some huge holes. And they're fast, too. I'm just looking for them to make a block. They make a block, I look to cut."

And Hunter can already cut with the best of them. He has made plenty of defenders look silly.

"He has some great speed and he can spring some plays, and he's tough to bring down," said Moyer, who completed eight of 14 passes for 106 yards.

And he's just a sophomore.

"He really hasn't turned on all of his speed yet," Williams said. "He's showing you a little bit. He's shifty. But only as he gets stronger will he use his power to break more tackles."

Hunter has gotten much stronger as the season has progressed. While most guys lose weight during a grueling 10-week season, Hunter has actually gained 18 pounds. He weighed 182 in August. He weighed 200 earlier this week.

"I'm blessed," Hunter said. "I'm just very, very blessed."

He's a tireless worker, too. His dad was an All-State safety and running back at York High. His son has inherited his work ethic.

"My dad taught me everything I know," Hunter said. "How to hold the ball. How to run with the ball. How to make cuts. And then I came to this school. This place is like a powerhouse. I wanted to learn a lot, especially from these coaches.

"These guys are doing a great job coaching. I've learned a lot of things here. Now I want to get bigger, get stronger and get faster."

And the Barons want to keep winning.

"These seniors do not want to lose," Hunter said. "They did not want a repeat of last season. So they've gone around and asked all of us to start stepping it up."

Hunter stepped it up on the biggest stage he's performed on in his brief career. And you get the feeling it won't be the last time.

Nov. 15:

Barons of the district once again

Central blitzes Lower Dauphin for title, 38-0

By Ed Gruver
Intelligencer Journal

HERSHEY — As Manheim Central senior captains Mike Byrne, Ryan Dennes, Neil Hershey and Jarryd Moyer strode toward midfield Friday night to collect their District Three Class AAA championship trophy, the voice of one Baron teammate rose above all others.

"Bring it home!"

Riding a devastating defense that forced four turnovers resulting in 28 points, Central reclaimed the Class

AAA title it had held for 10 straight seasons from 1992-2001 by dominating defending champion Lower Dauphin 38-0 at wind-swept Hersheypark Stadium.

"We dominated them up front and that was the key," said Barons head coach Mike Williams, whose team has now won 11 of the last 12 AAA titles, 13 overall since 1989 and is 27-3 in the district playoffs. "The key was putting pressure on them."

Central's unrelenting pressure yielded four sacks of Falcons senior QB Matt Ruffner and limited the Mid-Penn Conference Capital Division co-champs to 103 yards of total offense and just two trips inside Baron territory.

Lower Dauphin never advanced beyond the Barons' 31-yard line and by game's end had become Central's sixth shutout victim this season.

The victory advances the Barons (12-0) to next weekend's opening round of the PIAA playoffs opposite District Four champion Shamokin, a 17-3 winner Friday night over Selinsgrove. The win also allows Central to even an old score with Lower Dauphin. The Falcons (10-2) stunned the Barons 42-40 in last season's district opener on Ruffner's final-play touchdown pass.

"We probably thought a little bit about revenge," said Moyer, who rushed for 69 yards and one touchdown. "But we wanted to make a statement and I think we did."

Central controlled every phase of the game. Led by sophomore back Jeremiha Hunter, who ran for a game-high 141 yards on 17 carries, the Barons gouged out 323 yards of terra firma on 51 carries. Senior back Eric Meyers added 61 yards on nine carries and junior Craig Gatchell pounded out 40 yards and two TDs on 10 carries.

"Our line did a great job," said Hunter, paying tribute to Byrne, twin brothers Neil and Kevin Hershey, Rob Trovato and Ty Leese. "They were blowing them off the ball."

Falcons coach Rob Klock cited Central's line play as one of the key differences between this Barons team and last year's edition.

"They controlled both sides of the line of scrimmage," Klock said. "They're a lot better on the line than they were before. They've improved tremendously."

Central took control at the outset, driving 69 yards in eight plays on its opening possession. Hunter, who had 99 yards rushing in the first quarter and 109 in the half, highlighted the march by springing free on inside traps for gains of 32 and 17 yards.

Ryan Plowman's 22-yard field goal with 8:35 left in the first quarter gave Central a 3-0 lead, and the Barons increased their advantage to 10-0 on their next series when Moyer play-faked left, bootlegged right and scored on a fourth-and-goal from the 5.

Armed with a lead, Central's defense clamped down on Lower Dauphin. The Falcons didn't record their initial first down until the second play of the second quarter, which was also the first time Lower Dauphin moved into Manheim territory.

Seeking outside containment on Ruffner, the Barons collapsed the pocket and pressured Ruffner relentlessly, holding him to 74 yards passing and minus-6 yards rushing.

"Our defense really set the tempo for this game," Moyer said, and Klock agreed.

"No matter what we did, they adjusted well," he said. "We couldn't find any weaknesses."

Kevin Krause's forced fumble and Gatchell's recovery late in the second quarter led to Gatchell's first score of the game, a four-yard run off the left

side. The Barons made it 24-0 with 22 seconds left in the half when Kevin Hershey's sack of Ruffner jarred the ball loose at the 15 and defensive end Ryan Buchter recovered it in the end zone.

In the third, Nate Mast fell on a Ruffner fumble at the Falcons' 42, and six plays later Gatchell swept left and scored from the 2.

Mast's second recovery of a Falcon fumble led to Ben Engle's one-yard TD plunge with 21 seconds to go in the game, and all that remained for Central was to set its sights on a state title.

"We're tired of getting so far and losing," said Williams, referring to Central's frustrating PIAA defeats in years past. "Our goal is a state title, and we think this team can do it."

The Hershey twins separate Lower Dauphin quarterback Matt Ruffner from the ball.

Nov. 16:

Central: Is this finally the year?

Strath Haven, others stand between Manheim Central and a state Class AAA championship

By Mike Gross
Sunday News

The opposition changes, if not comprehensively, from year to year.

But as usual, Manheim Central is there.

The main obstacle and nemesis has, in recent years, moved 100 miles south, Strath Haven replacing Berwick.

Still, the Barons are there.

Central has earned 11 berths in the state playoffs, which have only existed since 1989. Six times, Central has reached the state semifinals.

No one has been this close, this often, through the entirety of the state-playoff era. But every time, the Barons have fallen short, the first three times to Berwick and the last three to Strath Haven.

Some of those games have been blowouts. Some have been thrillers. Some have involved plays and, yes, coaching decisions that will be recalled and debated for years.

It's November again, and Central is back, pawing at the turf and spoiling for another Sisyphean run up the mountain.

Is this the year?

"Each year is different," Central coach Mike Williams said Tuesday, even if, to outsiders, the similarities are more apparent.

"But as far as coaching techniques, work habits, what we expect from the kids and what they've given us, we haven't changed anything."

So is this the year?

"Believe me, we want it to be," said Mike Byrne, Central's superb two-way lineman.

That goes without saying. But are there, this time, specific reasons to believe?

A closer look, in four areas:

The opposition: There may not be a monster team in AAA comparable to Strath Haven in 1999 or the great Berwick teams. Still, Williams believes the AAA field is deeper than usual.

His scouts had seen Shamokin (11-1), which beat Selingsgrove 17-3 for the right to face Central, twice in person before this weekend.

The other half of the Eastern bracket: Pittston, which beat Wyoming Area 32-0 Saturday, vs. Strath Haven.

All those teams are solid, according to Williams, as are a few of the AAAs in the west, notably 11-0 Thomas Jefferson.

Wyoming eliminated Berwick two weeks ago, but ended with three losses. Strath Haven has reached the state final four straight years, and features an All-American class player in fullback-linebacker Dan Connor.

But Strath Haven has also lost tailback Phil Atkinson, a sprinter being recruited by several D-1s including Wisconsin, for the year to a knee injury.

"They're pretty talented," Williams said. "About like usual."

Central would run into Strath Haven in the semis, Nov. 28 or 29. Also like usual.

Deeee-fense: This unit has been a pleasant surprise to Williams and this year's biggest strength.

The Barons allowed 40 points in 10 regular-season games, then 15 in what was considered an uneven effort in last Friday's district opener against Hershey.

It's not just the numbers.

"They've gotten turnovers, made big plays and held us together when the offense was struggling," Williams said.

The Barons are big up front with the likes of the 6-5, 265-pound Byrne. They're quick and aggressive everywhere else with guys like sophomore linebacker Jeremiha Hunter and senior d-backs Shawn Wilt and Ryan Dennes.

The Hunter factor: Hunter is a transfer from York High, where he was a varsity player as a freshman.

At 6-2, 183 with sprinter's speed, Hunter gives the Barons what they haven't often had over the years, the super-gifted, breakaway back.

He's been part of a tailback-by-committee most of the year, but coming into this weekend Hunter had 365 yards the past two weeks.

"We tried not to put too much on him right away," Williams said. "No question, he's added a lot."

The leader: Central's best teams have usually had a gonzo-style leader, a guy — usually a fullback/linebacker — with a big personality who took care of a lot of the motivational stuff.

"A guy who's a little crazy," Williams said. "A guy who nobody messes with, who everybody's a little afraid of."

Last year, Corby Zeigler was that guy. Brad Barnett, the year before that. This year? No one, really.

It isn't quite in the nature of superb quarterback Jarryd Moyer. Nor of Byrne, perhaps Central's best all-around player and a brilliant student who turned down Ivy League looks to sign with the University of Delaware.

Byrne isn't sure it matters.

"We definitely don't have a guy like (Zeigler)," he said. "He was crazy, and he was a great teammate.

"But I don't know if you have to have that animal guy. I think this year, we're kind of knit together better. We don't have to yell at each other."

Nov. 22:

Central smokes Shamokin

By Jeffrey Reinhart
Lancaster New Era

MOUNT CARMEL — Note to Manheim Central football opponents:

Don't give the Barons any added ammunition.

Shamokin sure did when some of its players bragged about the Indians' defense leading up to Friday night's state Triple-A quarterfinal against Central.

Big mistake.

"They did a little too much talking in the newspapers up here," Central coach Mike Williams said. "And I think that got our kids fired up."

And then some.

Playing Central, the second-ranked Triple-A team in the state, is tough enough. Playing against a Central team that has some added motivation usually spells big trouble.

It did for Shamokin.

Central held the Indians to 58 yards of total offense and didn't allow the District 4 champs to cross midfield. And the Barons made mincemeat out of Shamokin's defense, churning out 145 yards on the ground and 309 yards total in Central's 50-0 victory in Mount Carmel High School's Silver Bowl Stadium.

Shamokin was allowing just 8.8 points a game.

"We saw all the papers and what they said about their defense," Williams said. "I thought we felt kind of slighted by that. So we pasted that stuff up all over our locker room, and I think that got our kids fired up."

Fired up enough to post the second-most-lopsided victory in the history of the state Triple-A playoffs. Last year, Perry Traditional Academy topped Clearfield Area 61-0 in a first-round game.

Friday night's win was Central's seventh shutout victory in 13 games, all of which the Barons have won. Central has won three of its last four games via shutout and has outscored its opponents 490-53. The Barons also improved to 6-10 in the state playoffs.

"I think it bothered us a little bit that they were talking a lot about their defense," Central senior wideout/defensive back Ryan Dennes said. "Hey, our stats were just as good. So we wanted to come out and make a statement, and I think we did that."

Central quarterback Jarryd Moyer made a statement of his own. The 6-4, 205-pound senior completed nine of 12 passes for 164 yards and accounted for six of Central's seven touchdowns.

Moyer tossed four touchdown passes — two to Dennes and one each to junior halfback Craig Gatchell and

senior tight end Tyler McCauley —
and had TD runs of 1 yard and 6
yards, respectively, as the Barons dominated the Indians (11-2) in absolutely
every phase of the game.

"It was no contest," Shamokin
coach Carm DeFrancesco said. "That's
a great football team. They dismantled
us. Sure, we made it easy for them, but
it wouldn't have mattered. We needed
to play an absolute perfect game to
beat that team."

Instead, Central, the District 3 and
Lancaster-Lebanon League Section 2
champ, played a near-perfect game to
set up another showdown against District 1 champ Strath Haven. The Panthers improved to 13-0 Friday night
with a 49-0 romp past Wyoming Area
in the other Eastern semifinal game.

Central and Strath Haven, the top-
ranked Triple-A team in the state, will
lock horns for the fourth time in a state
semifinal game Saturday at 1 p.m. at
Coatesville High School. The Panthers,
who knocked Central out of the state
playoffs in 1999, 2000 and 2001, have
appeared in the last four state championship games. They won state titles in
1999 and 2000.

"We feel like we can win, just like
Strath Haven feels it can win," Williams said. "Strath Haven is the elite
team in Pennsylvania, but it's about
time somebody has five fumbles
against us or drops the pass or does
this or does that. Everything that can
go wrong, usually does go wrong
against us in these games.

"It's time we put everything together."

"This is the game we've been waiting for our whole life," said McCauley,
who opened the scoring with 5:18 to
go in the first quarter Friday night
when he decked Shamokin senior
halfback Rich Schiccatano in the end
zone for a safety and a 2-0 Central
lead.

"Nobody blocked me," McCauley
said. "That play really got us going.
We got to the sideline, and everyone
was like, "That's the spark we needed.'
After that, we were ready to go."

Later in the first quarter, Moyer
zipped the first of his four TD passes,
an 8-yard strike to Gatchell that gave
the Barons a 9-0 lead with 49 seconds
to go in the quarter. Moyer sidestepped a pair of defenders and found
Gatchell, who made a nice shoestring
catch.

Central capitalized on a pair of
Shamokin fumbles to score a pair of
touchdowns in less than two minutes
in the second quarter. After Gatchell
recovered Schiccatano's fumble, Moyer
hit Dennes on a slant pattern for a 16-
yard score to make it 16-0 with 10:51 to
go in the half.

On the first play of Shamokin's
ensuing drive, senior halfback Dan
Wilk fumbled and Central sophomore
linebacker Jeremiha Hunter recovered at the Indians' 43. Four plays
later, Moyer lobbed a perfect fade to
Dennes, who scored from 29 yards out
to make it 23-0 with 9:16 to go in the

first half.

Central made it 30-0 with 4:17 to go in the second quarter when Moyer slammed in from a yard out. Dennes set that drive up with a 26-yard punt return.

"They loaded the box, so we wanted to spread things out with the passing game," said Dennes, who had four catches for 101 yards, including a 49-yard reception that set up Moyer's final TD toss, a 3-yard lob to McCauley that made it 37-0 with 4:41 to go in the third quarter.

Later in the quarter, after Central sophomore linebacker Nate Mast recovered Shamokin's third fumble, Moyer darted in from the 6 on fourth-and-goal to make it 44-0 with 1:52 to go. After Central junior defensive back Tyler Swarr picked off Wes Griffiths' pass midway through the fourth quarter, senior halfback Ben Engle capped the scoring with an 11-yard run with 1:25 to play.

Griffiths, a 5-11, 160-pound junior, had a forgettable game against the Barons. He completed just 3 of 13 passes for 11 yards and was sacked five times — twice by senior tackle Kevin Hershey — for minus-12 yards. The Indians rushed 24 times for 47 yards. That's a woeful 1.9 yards a carry.

"They were sort of bragging about their defense," Moyer said. "So our defense wanted to make a statement. They did a great job."

Shamokin didn't get a first down until its second play of the third quarter after gaining just eight yards — none for a first down — on 15 plays in the first half.

Central's defense was that good.

"Everyone was saying that this was going to be a battle of the defenses," McCauley said. "And I think we showed them who we are."

The Barons hope to do the same against Strath Haven.

Nov. 23:

Central finds inspiration in coal regions

By Mike Gross
Sunday News

MOUNT CARMEL — Manheim Central football coach Mike Williams looks everywhere for motivation.

He found some in Schuylkill County newspapers last week, where there were tales of the suffocating defense of Shamokin, Central's opponent in Friday's first round of the state Class AAA football playoffs.

"We read some of that stuff to the kids at practice," Williams said. "We had it up on the locker-room wall."

He found more when he walked into Mount Carmel High School, venue for Friday's game, evidence of five state AA championships in the trophy case.

"Very impressive," Williams said. "Very inspiring."

Then there was the agreeably gritty atmosphere at Mount Carmel's famous Silver Bowl, with a graveyard, a supermarket, an auto-repair place, a bar and an assisted-living facility all within a John Elway bomb of the 50-yard line.

Only Shamokin wasn't up to the occasion.

The coal regions are famous for high-school football, and for the fourth time since 1999, Manheim Central faced one of its teams in the first round of states.

Like the others it was an odd game. Like the others Shamokin could do one thing — defend the run, in this case — at least as well as the Barons. And like the others, the Indians seemed bewildered by a team that could do as many things as well as Central.

Like the others, it was a Central win that put the Barons within comfortable dreaming distance of their first, and epically elusive, state title.

Again, though, Shamokin did have a defense; quick, athletic, and tough. So tough, in fact, that it might not have needed nine defenders within inches of the line of scrimmage, but that's the way coach Carmen DeFrancesco

played it because that's how he always plays it.

Knowing that, Williams scripted his team's first 10 offensive plays with the pass in mind. The play-action pass, in particular.

"You can't run against 11 guys like that," Williams said. "The way they were rolling their cornerbacks and safeties up so close, they were giving us something. We had to take it."

So it began with Central quarterback Jarryd Moyer in the shotgun formation. He was sacked perhaps a second after taking the game's first snap by a linebacker who appeared to be blitzing, but probably was just doing what he always does.

It took Central a little time to get going. The teams traded punts, but Central's second one, by Jeremy Smith, landed on the Shamokin 1-yard line and sucked back like a Phil Mickelson L-wedge, settling at the Shamokin 3.

On the first play from there Central's Tyler McCauley smothered Shamokin tailback Rich Schiccatano three yards deep in the end zone for a ridiculously easy safety.

Eric Meyers returned the ensuing kickoff to the Shamokin 44 and from there to halftime, at which point the issue was long decided, the game was played on the shortest field since Coors Field.

Central started its next three drives on the Shamokin 44, the Shamokin 44 and the Shamokin 30. Touchdown, touchdown, touchdown.

By halftime it was 30-0. By the final gun it was 50-0, and the caravan down I-81 was well under way.

It wouldn't be precisely accurate to say that Moyer had to make throws, because it would probably have taken Shamokin several days to score against Central's defense.

But it would be accurate to say Moyer made some great ones. Like the 16-yard slant he gunned over the middle to Ryan Dennis for a touchdown in what was a classic football play: great coverage, great throw, great catch.

That made it 16-0. Then there was the deep post Moyer laid perfectly in Dennes' arms to make it 23-0.

For the game, Moyer was 9-12 for 164 yards, or 13.6 yards per pass play. Moyer threw for four TDs, no interceptions, and ran for two others.

"I was definitely nervous at the beginning," said Moyer, who is probably going to be a Division I-AA scholarship player, perhaps at Delaware.

"Then I got sacked right away, but I didn't let it bother me. I guess it was my best game this year."

Moyer is self-effacing. DeFrancesco went much further: "He's as good a quarterback as I've ever seen."

Again, though, the Barons could have done without him. That's because of a defense that held Shamokin to minus-9 yards rushing in the first half, that didn't allow a first down until the third quarter, that didn't allow Shamokin past the 50-yard line.

The defense that wasn't very good a year ago, and has come so far since, might hold the Barons' best hope of scaling Strath Haven. The state semifinal is tentatively scheduled for 1 p.m. Saturday at Coatesville High School.

Two years ago, Central held Strath Haven to 105 total yards and no second-half first downs in a now infamous and gut-wrenching 14-13 loss.

"That was a great defense," John Brubaker, Central defensive coordinator, said Saturday.

"This one is showing signs of playing that well.

"Last year we had some growing pains. This year we've had some kids who didn't play last year, or who did play but not well, really come through for us."

Brubaker singled out Shawn Wilt, a senior free safety who has become a defensive leader.

"We wanted to get him involved last year, but he just wasn't ready," Brubaker said. "He's a real vocal kid, he recognizes things, gets us into the right adjustments. He's really stepped up."

This week, of course, is another matter. There is no chance of bewildering Strath Haven.

"The next two weeks are going to require a lot of learning, a lot of intensity, and tremendous dedication," Brubaker said. "I think our kids are ready for it."

Note that Central has been to the state semis seven times before, and is 0-7.

Note also that Brubaker said two weeks.

Tracy Buchter, left,
her son Ryan Buchter,
below, and Ty Leese
(52) celebrate the
exorcising of ghosts.

Archives III:
The Strath Haven Game

Nov. 28:

Mutual respect is clear

Haven, Barons have much in common

By Ed Gruver
Intelligencer Journal

They run drills into the night, pushing themselves through the harsh demands of practice to prepare for the harsher demands that will come with Saturday's PIAA Class AAA Eastern Final.

And it would seem to matter little if you're at Elden Rettew Field in Manheim or Strath Haven's George L. King Field, it's very likely the scene is the same. The Barons and Panthers enter the 1 p.m. state semifinal at Coatesville High with identical 13-0 records, similar histories, matched traditions and a shared respect.

"Both schools are similar in a lot of ways," Panthers head coach Kevin Clancy opined. "Both teams have a lot of tradition and both play with a lot of heart."

There are other similarities as well. The two coaches, Clancy and Manheim Central's Mike Williams, share a high regard for one another. They coached together at the 2000 East-West All-Star Game in Altoona.

Clancy is impressed by the high-tech aspect of the Barons' offense. Williams has respect for Clancy's fundamental approach to the game. The Barons' boss is even more impressed by the way Clancy carries himself.

"Kevin is proof," Williams said,

"that nice guys can finish first."

Both programs have a familial feel about them. Central's offensive and defensive fronts feature the Hershey twins, Neil and Kevin. Strath Haven guard/linebacker Sam McGarity's older brother Owen captained the Panthers' 2001 team, and his younger brother Mike is a junior guard/linebacker this season. Fullback/linebacker Dan Connor's older brothers, Jim and Mike, both played for the Panthers.

"I noticed some names on Manheim's roster that looked familiar," Clancy said. Both teams, he added, are alike in that they have younger brothers and cousins who grew up close to the program, watching their older relatives play, and are now a part of the team themselves.

"There's a lot of tradition at both schools," Clancy said, "and a lot of these kids have seen it at home and understand it."

While their playing styles differ — the Barons are option-oriented on offense; the Panthers favor the power game — opposing coaches see a noticeable likeness.

In the wake of last week's 50-0 loss to Central in their state playoff opener, Shamokin coach Carmen DeFrancesco said he was surprised by the Barons' physical size and quickness.

"We had no idea (what Central was like physically)," he said. "They're much bigger, stronger and faster than they looked on film."

Strath Haven's opponents have

Mike Williams felt his team was overdue.

been uttering similar quotes this season. Having fallen 49-0 to the Panthers last week, Wyoming Area coach Paul Marranca told The Citizen's Voice newspaper that his team was overwhelmed by the Panthers' size and strength.

"Outmanned and beat up," is how Marranca termed it.

Size and strength aside, the most common thread between Central and Strath Haven is, of course, the success of their respective programs.

The Barons have claimed 13 District Three Class AAA titles, including 11 of the last 12 and 10 straight from 1992-2001.

The Panthers own nine District One AAA championships, including eight in a row dating back to 1996.

Central has won 16 Lancaster-Lebanon League Section Two titles, and nine of 12 dating back to 1992.

The Panthers have 10 Central League championships, eight straight from 1996-03.

Similarities exist. But one thing seems certain. Come Saturday, these two programs that have so much alike will have major differences to settle on the field.

Nov. 28:

Inspiration Central

Smoker's pep talk fires up Barons...

By Jeffrey Reinhart
Lancaster New Era

While your turkey was roasting in the oven Thursday morning, Manheim Central's football players strapped on their shoulder pads and helmets and hit the field for a pre-feast practice.

But this wasn't your average, run-of-the-mill practice.

This practice was for Saturday's 1 p.m. state Triple-A semifinal game at Coatesville High School against mighty Strath Haven, the top-ranked team in the state. And the team that knocked Central out of the state play-offs in 1999, 2000 and 2001.

This practice was to fine-tune the Barons' game plan. To work out some last-minute kinks and make sure everyone and everything is in perfect working order for Saturday's showdown, which will be telecast on WGCB-TV 49 and broadcast on 1490 WLPA-AM.

This practice, in coach Mike Williams' mind, was so important that he called in one of Manheim's favorite sons to give his team a little pep talk. But not just any pep talk. This pep talk, Williams thought, would be the pep talk of all pep talks. The mother of all pep talks. The pep talk that

Jeff Smoker told the Barons to make sure this game wasn't their last.

would inspire his team to play like a champion on Saturday and become the first team from Central to advance to the state title game.

There's only one guy who could deliver that kind of a pep talk. And that guy was Jeff Smoker. The former Central star and Michigan State's senior quarterback, in town to visit family and friends for Thanksgiving, delivered an inspired pep talk after practice Thursday morning.

"Jeff didn't have to say anything at all, really," Williams said. "Just his presence was awesome. If we win this game, it'll be a victory for the whole program. For all the kids who made all the sacrifices before these guys.

"It'll be for every kid who ever played for us."

Including Smoker, who was more than happy to do this favor for his former coach.

Only time will tell if Smoker's speech was the one that helped get Central into the state title game. But Thursday morning, with a throng of players and coaches listening, Smoker, flanked by his brothers, Bob and Craig, and by another former Central star quarterback, University of Delaware grad Matt Nagy, sure got everyone fired up.

"You guys know what's at stake," Smoker told the team, which was kneeling in front of him, glued to his every word. "You know what's on the line. All I can tell you to do is to make the most of it. Make sure this isn't your last game."

Central, the 13-time District 3 Triple-A champ, is 0-8 in this game. The Barons are 0-5 against Berwick and 0-3 against Strath Haven in the Eastern championship. There have been blowouts. There have been squeakers. There have been heartbreakers. The 14-13 loss to Strath Haven in 2001, when the Barons went for but didn't convert a two-point conversion in the game's final minute, would qualify as the No. 1 heartbreaker.

But there have been zero victories by the Barons in a state semifinal game.

Smoker, who graduated in 2000, told the players to forget about that history and make a little history of their own.

"There's a lot of history here. And a lot of tradition," Smoker said. "But the only thing we don't have here is a state title. We want the 2003 Barons to bring home that state title. I want you to think about that.

"I want you to think about beating Strath Haven. And I want you to think about winning the game after that. Think about winning that state title. If you win the state title, you guys will be remembered forever. So go out there Saturday and play your hearts out. I'll be there watching. The whole town will be there watching. And all of us will be pulling for you.

"I even know a bunch of people up at Michigan State who are pulling for you."

All of that support, including Smoker's, can only help.

"Everybody has a lot of respect for Smoker around here," said Central senior center/defensive end Mike Byrne, who recently made a verbal commitment to accept a full athletic scholarship offer from Division I-AA Delaware. "And it was great for him to come back here. It's pretty inspiring. Jeff is a great quarterback, but he never won a state title here. But he's right. Everyone in town is backing us, and we really want to make it happen on Saturday."

In order for that to happen, Smoker told the players, they must dig deep and play for each other. Play for the town. Play with pride and with passion. And play for everyone who played for the Barons before them.

"Play for the guy beside you," Smoker said. "Play for your friends. Play for your family. Play for your school. Give it all you've got. Make sure when you wear that maroon and gray, you wear it with pride. I wore it with pride. My brothers wore it with pride. Nagy wore it with pride.

"Every time we put on that maroon and gray, we laid it all out on the line with blood, sweat and tears for each other. That's what you guys need to do. And whatever you do, don't walk off that field without knowing you gave it all you had. And I'm not even going to say win or lose, because there is no losing. Manheim doesn't lose. Nobody beats the Barons.

"So good luck, and go get 'em."

Cheers went up. Fists were pumped. Roars were heard. And everyone had a smile and a handshake for Smoker, who went 30-4 as a starting quarterback for the Barons before he headed to Michigan State.

"That was great," Central senior quarterback Jarryd Moyer said. "It's cool that he was here and knowing that he's going to be there for us. He's a great leader. He was down, but he picked himself up. I know we can do that, too. We just have to play our game. We can't be afraid of them. We have to come out and stick them."

Nov. 30:

BELIEVE IT!

On its ninth visit to the Eastern final, Manheim Central finally topples Strath Haven

By Mike Gross
Sunday News

COATESVILLE — Delirium.

Not only that, but well-earned delirium. The best kind.

It's source: the hurdle Manhein Central cleared Saturday, a hurdle so huge and historic that it's hard to believe this story must have another chapter.

But it must. For the first time in Central's proud football history, the Barons are in their sport's ultimate game.

Central exorcized the ghosts of eight state-semifinal losses with a 3-0 defeat of Strath Haven to win the Class AAA Eastern Championship before a packed house Saturday at Coatesville High School.

"Eight is enough," Central coach Mike Williams said. "We put everything we had into this."

They did it by beating a power team in a power game necessitated by conditions suitable only for indoor sports.

"It was the greatest win in Manheim Central history, ever," said Central safety Shawn Wilt, although that

pretty much went without saying.

It means Central (14-0) faces Western champ Pine-Richland for the big prize at 7 p.m. Friday at Hersheypark Stadium.

It means Central's tradition of agonizing near-misses at the highest level of high-school football is over.

The Barons had been 0-8 in state semifinals, three of the losses to Strath Haven, which had emerged as the state's top AAA power.

With straight-ahead power football, Strath Haven took a brutally simple path to that status. That was the only approach possible Saturday, thanks to near-freezing temperatures, awful field conditions and, most importantly, a howling 40 mph wind.

But Central beat the Panthers at their own game, scoring a decisive victory in the battle of the line of scrimmage.

"That's the best line we've played all year," said Strath Haven coach Kevin Clancy, whose team epitomized class in defeat.

"They just outmanned us," said Dan Connor, Strath Haven's Penn

State-bound fullback/linebacker. "They did an unbelievable job. They're on a mission; I have them winning it all."

The winning points came on Ryan Plowman's 25-yard field goal early in the second quarter.

Those three points were the only tangible benefit from a first half in which Central ran 42 offensive plays to the Panthers' 12 and had drives of 7:04, 5:50 and 6:33.

Those numbers, more than the score, tell you what needs to be known about Central's defense and offensive front.

"Our line was unbelievable today," quarterback Jarryd Moyer said. "They won it for us."

In a game where inches were like yards, first downs were like points and field position was everything, Central moved the chains 11 times before half-time, riding sophomore running back Jeremiha Hunter hard.

Hunter finished with 115 yards in 23 carries. The yards gained by quarterback Jarryd Moyer and RB Eric Meyers, 54 and 43, were just as big, for chain-moving purposes.

The defense held the Panthers to 80 total yards, ganged up on Connor enough to keep him to 50 yards on 13 tries, and forced two turnovers to Central's inconsequential one.

Central had the wind in the fourth quarter, which meant it had to nurse its tiny lead through the third quarter playing it as close to the vest as pos-sible.

The Barons' first punt of the game came in the middle of the third, the wind at its howlingest. It went five yards.

Strath Haven took over at the Barons' 39, and Connor immediately rumbled nine yards, his biggest gain of the day.

The Panthers needed all four downs to move those chains. On first down from the 28, Wilt intercepted an underthrown ball by Strath Haven QB Rick Coppick.

The Panthers got it back and rode Connor to the Central 30 before stall-ing, crucially committing a delay of game penalty in a game that was mostly mistake-free.

Then there was punt trading, until Strath Haven took over for what fig-ured to be one last try with 5:32 left.

On third-and-nine from the 33, Coppick hit Connor with a swing pass, and he rumbled into Central territory, where he met up with Central's Craig Gatchell.

"I knew he had the first down anyway," Gatchell said, "so I went for the ball."

He got it, prying it loose from Con-nor. The resourceful Wilt fell on it.

It was Strath Haven's first complet-ed pass, the first time it tried to throw to Connor.

"I was thinking about a long run, trying to make something happen," Connor said. "I lost focus."

Still, 4:38 remained. Central converted a huge third-and-six on a quick hitter up the middle by Meyers.

Then Hunter carried Panthers seven yards and finally, Strath Haven seemed worn down and beat.

Nate Mast got the first down on his only carry. Moyer went nine yards. A play later, Hunter got the first down that sealed it.

All that remained was Moyer taking a knee, and the final gun, and the hugs, for and from Barons past and present.

It was a game a lineman could love, but only a Manheim Central lineman. Mike Byrne, for example, the Barons' center of whom Connor said, "I butted heads with him a lot ... he's a great, great player."

Also a happy one.

"We just pounded the ball the whole game," he said. "It was a fun game, now that I think about it."

Pounded the ball. Pounded the Panthers. Pounded the ghosts.

Delirium. Well earned.

Nov. 30:

This year's Barons have the 'X factor'

By Mike Gross
Sunday News

COATESVILLE — Mike Williams is not Knute Rockne.

The Manheim Central coach doesn't normally get emotional in his pre-game speech to his players. He couldn't help it Saturday.

"I told them they were the lucky ones," Williams said. "I told them they had a chance to do it for everybody that's come through our program. It's our time."

The current Barons have reached so high, of course, by standing on the shoulders of their predecessors.

But Williams knew this team was different. It was the biggest he's had in 23 years at the Central helm. The most physically powerful.

It was as good as any he's had defensively.

These Barons have a quarterback, Jarryd Moyer, in the Central tradition of Smoker and Nagy but don't utterly depend on him.

Further, these Barons have the X factor, the big, powerful, athletic kid that had genetic stuff you can't teach.

That would be sophomore running back/linebacker Jeremiha Hunter, a transfer from York.

"In other years, I always felt like we were a player short," Williams said, remembering kids like Strath Haven's Mark Jones, a fleet receiver, d-back and kick returner who attended the University of Tennessee.

"We're glad Jeremiha moved to our town," Williams said. "He's a phenomenal sophomore."

Still, Strath Haven was Strath Haven, a state champion twice and finalist four times since 1999.

And as Williams prepared for Saturday's Class AAA state semifinal against the Panthers, the weather forecast scared him as much as the opponent.

Severe rain came Friday night and soaked the Coatesville High School field. Saturday was freezing cold, with winds gusting to near tornado force.

Throwing the ball on a day like Saturday could be like playing the lottery. Running it wouldn't be much easier.

It meant football became a land-acquisition game played by plodding infantry.

It meant punts would be wild adventures. It meant a whole new approach to play-calling and down-and-distance management.

It meant the game would be played at Strath Haven's favored pace and style, and without some of Central's ammo.

"It was a hard game to coach," Williams said as the wind howled.

"It was harder to play in; I think the college and pros would have a hard time playing in this."

Williams figured it out quickly. He scrapped the option game on offense and played very, very conservatively.

"We really only ran two plays," said center Mike Bryne, overstating just a little. "Power and dive."

Power and dive were mostly good for three yards and a clump of mud, over and over and over.

Central's first drive was 14 plays and over seven minutes long. It ended on an interception when Moyer tried to force a ball on a fourth-down play. The pick actually cost Strath Haven nine yards and on this day, yards were gold.

"I think the first drive of the game (was the difference)," Strath Haven coach Kevin Clancy said.

It probably wasn't the whole difference, but it showed Central could block the Panthers. The Barons ultimately rushed for 223 yards to Strath Haven's 68.

But Central wasn't just chasing its ghosts Saturday. Williams was chasing his, ghosts he alluded to last week when he wondered if maybe, this would finally be the year that "the other coach makes a bad decision."

Williams went for two in the final minute of the state semis two years ago when a PAT would have meant overtime, and Strath Haven beat Central, 14-13.

Up 17-0 in 1995, he could have kicked a field goal at the end of the first half of the semis, and maybe buried Berwick. Instead he went for the TD. Berwick 18, Central 17.

And so on.

The ghosts didn't scare him Saturday.

Early in the second quarter, Williams could have tried a 32-yard field goal but went for, and converted, a fourth-down-and-four instead.

Central went for four fourth downs and converted three. Which was less risky than it sounds. Behind every move Williams made Saturday was a bottomless belief in his defense, a belief that allowed him to ride a 3-0, second-quarter lead like it was Secretariat.

"That's exactly right," he said. "A lot of teams talk about their defense. Ours is pretty good, too."

The ghosts did get his attention one last time. This was at halftime, when the officials came in the locker room to ask if he wanted the wind in the fourth quarter or the third.

He took the fourth. Then he stayed in the locker room for a long moment, after everyone else had gone.

"I was shaking my head for a long time," he said.

Later he went for a fourth-and-one on his own 11, which seems insane unless you know that a few moments

earlier, into the wind, Central had punted the ball five yards.

Again, the Barons converted.

A few minutes later the third quarter was over, it was still 3-0, and the Barons had the wind the rest of the way.

Good call, coach.

Williams got 115 yards in 23 tries from Hunter, who is going to be a flat-out monster.

But he saved gutsy senior Eric Meyers for the perfect moments, such as the 6-yard quick opener up the middle that moved the chains at a decisive time in the final minutes.

One first down later, Strath Haven was beaten. No comebacks this time. No second-guessing. Or first-guessing. Or third.

Then there was a lot of emotion. And perhaps a half hour and a half-dozen interviews later, Williams was able to acknowledge what it meant.

"I sort of felt like if we didn't do it this time, we might never see it, with me as the head coach," he said.

"This game was it for everybody," he said. "We prepared for this so hard, and so much."

And now they get to do it all over again. Friday at Hershey.

Ghostless.

Nov. 30:

Fans young and old live the dream

By Eric Stark
Sunday News

COATESVILLE — Joe Grimm sat bundled up on the left side of the metal bleachers at Coatesville High School Saturday.

The brisk wind, which reached 45 mph at times, would not deter him from a front-row seat for Manheim Central's latest try at a state title.

The 1978 Manheim Central graduate said he has endured Friday nights and Saturday afternoons like this before. The late-November weather was easier to handle than the Barons' previous eight appearances in the Eastern state final.

Each of those ended in close losses.

"It's unbelievable," he said. "It's just terrible. It leaves such a bad taste in your mouth. (The coaches) ask so much of the players and they get so close. It almost makes you not want to come back next time. Almost."

Grimm was glad he was there Saturday, as the ninth time proved to be the charm for Manheim Central, which defeated Strath Haven 3-0 to earn its first appearance in the state final Friday night in Hersheypark Stadium against Pine-Richland.

Central is only the second Lancaster County team to reach the state final in football. Conestoga Valley lost to Erie Strong-Vincent in 1991.

Early in the fourth quarter, Sheri Byrne said the 3-0 score made her nervous. Normally at this point in the game, she said, Central has scored more than three points and has developed a bit of a cushion.

"It's nerve-wracking," said Byrne, whose son, Mike, starts at center. "I'm not a nervous mom, but last night I woke up with thoughts of this game in my head. You see what the kids go through and you want them to make it to the state final. When they come this far and you see their dream, you want them to go even further."

With 4:38 to play in the game, she said the Baron players were a little closer to realizing their dream was coming true.

Byrne is part of a group of five or six Central football moms known as "The Dark Side," a nickname that started when many of the current Baron players were playing junior-high-school football. These mothers are noted for being very verbal at games.

Tracy Buchter, wearing her son Ryan's No. 57 jersey, said she is the president of "The Dark Side." Usually she does not become nervous until Thursday when Central plays a game, but she said she became nervous Monday in anticipation of the Strath

Shawn Wilt celebrates yet another game-changing play, an end-zone interception vs. Strath Haven.

Haven clash, the fourth time the two teams have met in the Eastern state final with a berth in the state final on the line.

She said she did not sleep Friday night, but neither did Ryan, who was running a fever of 102 degrees. Five Central players played the game with a virus and were running high temperatures, she said. Quarterback Jarryd Moyer told a friend after the game that his temperature was down to 99 degrees at the beginning of the game.

Moyer's 11-year-old brother, Chase, wore a maroon No. 10 jersey (his brother's number) and a big smile after the game. He said he was

nervous at the beginning of the game and began getting pumped up as he watched the scoreboard clock.

"I was just thinking they were doing a great job," he said, "that they should keep their soul in the game and just keep fighting to the end."

They did just that, much to the delight of Mike Connelly, who was a lineman at Manheim Central in the 1960s and has been an avid fan.

"Finally," he said. "They always had good teams, but this one played well together. There are no real stars; everyone just did their part. They have been working on this state championship since last year when they got knocked out of the district playoffs."

Senior Anna Ludwig, who is the Manheim Central Baron mascot, realized just how tense this game was when no one asked her to do push-ups to tally Central's score, a tradition the Baron usually performs between the third and fourth quarters.

"I guess it wasn't enough points," Ludwig said. "It was amazing how they worked together and came together."

Ludwig said she turned to a friend during the game and said, "Wouldn't it be great if we won by three?"

Oh, my gosh, I was so nervous," Danielle Forward, a sophomore Baron cheerleader, said. "I am speechless. I can't wait until Friday night."

Neither can the rest of Manheim Central's fans.

"Friday night at 7 we'll be there yelling and have no voice by Saturday," Buchter said. "They (the players) wanted this so bad and they are just a great group of guys."

Former Baron quarterback Jeff Smoker, a senior playing football at Michigan State, watched the game from the sideline Saturday. He said he did not know this team personally, but was impressed and said head coach Mike Williams deserves a lot of credit.

"They looked really good," Smoker said about this year's squad, "as good as any team of the past."

No, this team is one game better.

Archives IV:

The Pine-Richland Game

Dec. 2:

Williams guards against letdown ...

Did the Barons leave everything they had out there on the muddy, wind-swept field at Coatesville High, or do they have enough left in the tank to go the final mile?

By Dennis Fisher
Lancaster New Era

They celebrated like there was no tomorrow. But there are three big tomorrows ahead.

They acted like it was the biggest win of their lives. But there is an even bigger win to be secured.

Manheim Central's players made history Saturday, when they became the first Barons to qualify for a state football championship game. With their 3-0 victory over Strath Haven they became the only football team in their school's history to get out of the state semifinals alive.

Before last Saturday, eight Baron powerhouses had marched into the state semis. And eight had limped back to Manheim with their heads bowed.

But last Saturday the Barons roared back home from Coatesville with their heads held high, their fists pumped skyward and a win over the top-ranked Triple-A team in the state in tow.

Ryan Huber, (with ball) is mobbed by teammates after completing the game's most remarkable play.

The victory was so monumental, so emotional, so long overdue that you have to wonder if they will have anything left for Friday's 7 p.m. championship game against Pine-Richland in Hersheypark Stadium.

Did they leave everything they had out there on the muddy, wind-swept field at Coatesville High against the top-ranked Triple-A team in the state, or do they still have enough left in the tank to go the final mile?

Is there a letdown on the horizon?

"That would only be natural," says Jim Cantafio, whose 1991 Conestoga Valley Buckskins previously were the only Lancaster County team that ever got to the state finals.

"Central got so close, so often. Now they know that win or lose Friday night they're still a winner, because they're the only team in Manheim Central history that got this far.

"You have a tendency to relax.

"After we beat Shamokin in the state semifinals, the next week I kept saying, "I can't believe we're in the state championship game.'

"I got a little satisfied. I didn't feel the pressure like I'd felt it the week before. The key is to keep that pressure up.

"I remember getting a letter from Gerry Slemmer (who was Wilson High's coach back then) that week. He wrote, "Don't be satisfied just to get there. Win the game or you'll be thinking about it for the rest of your life."

Cantafio's Buckskins didn't win their state title game, and he still thinks about it.

"I just watched a tape of our state final," he said Monday night. "I still get goosebumps."

And he still wishes he'd have found a way to keep the pressure up for that final week of the season.

"It's the most important game of your life," said the guy who is now Wilson's coach. "Central's players have to realize that."

Mike Williams realizes it.

"That was first and foremost on our minds at practice today," Manheim Central's coach said Monday night. "We spoke to our players about that very thing.

"We've had that problem in the past. I remember the year we beat Allentown Central Catholic when they were the No. 1-ranked team in the state. We got killed by Berwick in the next game.

"Over a 17-week season it's tough to sustain the kind of intensity you need to win a state title. At this point, words don't mean anything. You've got to have heart.

"This is a once-in-a-lifetime oportunity, and you've got to make the most of it."

Williams is doing his best to make sure his players do exactly that. He points out that they've been up to every challenge so far during this unblemished season. He sees nothing that might indicate that this week will go any differently than the previous

14, which all ended with Baron victories.

"It's early in the week, but I think our kids are starting to refocus," he says. "We've cleared a major hurdle and we've reached a mighty big plateau. We talked to the kids about not being satisfied, and we got some pretty positive looks.

"We had a moderate practice. It wasn't great and it wasn't terrible. As the week goes on, we'll really start grinding."

And, he hopes, the hunger will start grinding in their stomachs again.

Dec. 5:

Satisfied? Don't even think it

Barons know that without PIAA title, Eastern championship means little

By Ed Gruver
Intelligencer Journal

The Eastern Final is behind them, and longtime nemesis Strath Haven has been subdued.

Manheim Central (14-0), however, sounds anything but satisfied heading into tonight's PIAA Class AAA championship game — weather permitting — opposite Western champion Pine-Richland (14-0) at 7 p.m. at Hersheypark Stadium (PCN-TV; WLPA-AM 1490).

"It's totally the opposite (of satisfaction)," senior wide receiver/safety Shawn Wilt said. "Everybody that I've talked to on the team feels like that last game we won wasn't really a big deal.

"That (Eastern final) was a big hurdle because we had never gotten over it, but we don't even look at that as being a big game. Because if we don't win states, that (win over Strath Haven) doesn't mean anything."

As Wilt spoke, strains of Bon Jovi's "Livin' on a Prayer" blared from a locker room stereo. A good luck omen for the Barons? Maybe, but luck seems to have little to do with the way Central has been physically dominating opponents this season.

"They're the biggest team we'll have played this season," Rams head coach Clair Altemus said. "And the most physical.

"We're not that big, and we're not that physical, so it's kind of like David versus Goliath."

Pine-Richland may be at a size disadvantage along both fronts, but the

District Seven champs are not without power. Central coach Mike Williams and his staff have been impressed with Rams senior two-way tackle Greg Conti, who at 6-foot-1, 270 outweighs any of the Barons' starters up front.

"He's a wrestler (in the winter season) and he has amazing strength and balance," Altemus said. "He's the most dominating lineman I've been associated with in my 30 years of coaching."

Conti is joined in the middle of the Rams' defense by 6-4, 290-pound tackle Mike Nanna. Behind them is a linebacker foursome averaging 188 pounds per man, topped by 205-pound senior standout Greg Hough.

"It'll be a good matchup in the trenches, which is where state championship games are always won," Williams said. "It'll be interesting."

Other matchups beg attention as well.

Central's veer-option offense, which has produced 5,531 yards and 531 points this season, features a strong option runner in 6-4, 205-pound senior quarterback Jarryd Moyer. Moyer has rushed for 990 yards and 14 TDs this season, and thrown for 1,479 yards and an additional 15 scores against just five interceptions.

"He's a big, physical kid," Altemus said of Moyer. "I like him, he's tough. He's taken some tough shots and gotten right back up. He's a warrior."

Lining up behind Moyer in the backfield are senior Eric Meyers (760,

5.8, 12 TDs) and sophomore Jeremiha Hunter (1,225, 7.7, 14).

Wilt (20-436, 21.8, 2) and fellow senior Ryan Dennes (31-422, 13.6, 9) head the receiving corps.

Senior Mike Byrne (6-5, 265) is the linchpin of a highly-regarded line that includes the Hershey twins, Kevin and Neil, at guard and tackle, respectively. Senior tackle Rob Trovato and junior guard Ty Leese complete a line that Altemus said is more impressive than the dominating front fielded by state AAA champ Hopewell last season.

"Byrne is the leader of that whole group," said Altemus, and a key matchup on the line will be Central's inside triangle of Byrne and guards Kevin Hershey and Leese against massive defensive tackles Conti and Nanna.

Pine-Richland counters with a defense that has been Ram-tough, holding opponents to an average of 12.2 points per game and their last two state playoff opponents (Thomas Jefferson and Bradford) to seven points apiece.

"We want to keep the ball out of their hands," Altemus said. "They like to eat the clock with long drives, and that can be devastating to a defense."

To control the game's tempo offensively, the Rams look to an offense fronted by a line featuring Conti and pair of quick, 190-pound guards in Matt Sanders and Matt Piotrowski.

Jake Long, a sophomore transfer from Bradford, directs an offense

Ryan Dennes celebrates his punt-return touchdown during the Pine-Richland game.

averaging 36 points and 327 yards per game. Long has completed 59 percent of his passes (109-183) and thrown for 1,635 yards and 24 TDs with five picks.

Hough, who has rushed for close to 4,000 yards in his career, and 5-7, 150-pound senior Tim Newman key the ground game. In their state opener two weeks ago against Thomas Jefferson, both Hough (852, 8.5, 14) and Newman (1,244, 6.0, 15) rushed for more than 100 yards.

Senior Neil Walker, who owns a Division I baseball scholarship to Clemson, stars at wideout (66-1,084, 16.4, 18 TDs) and free safety. He and junior tight end Billy Massaro (26-316, 4 TDs) will be the primary concerns for a Barons secondary headed by Wilt, Dennes and senior Jeremy Smith, a secondary allowing an average of just 85 yards passing per game.

Central's senior-oriented 4-4, which is yielding an average of 85 yards rushing, features Byrne, Neil Hershey, Kevin Krause and Ryan Buchter. Hunter, Meyers, Craig Gatchell and Tyler McCauley comprise the linebacking corps.

"They're very talented," Williams said of the Rams. "They're coming out of a tough district, District Seven, which plays good football, so the battle will be for pride.

"Can our guys outmuscle theirs?

I think that really is what's going to determine the game, especially if we get the bad weather predicted.

"Run the football, play great defense and tackle. That's what's going to win you a state title."

Note: With a winter storm warning in effect for today and Saturday, an eight-team conference call will be held with PIAA officials this morning to determine the fate of the four state playoff finals scheduled to be held in Hershey this weekend.

Dec. 6:

Central reigns in the snow

Blocked kick in 2nd OT gives Barons state title

By Keith Schweigert
Lancaster New Era

HERSHEY — It was Manheim magical.

After enduring years of near-misses and frustration, Manheim Central's long quest for a state Triple-A football championship ended Friday night with a thrilling 39-38 double-overtime victory over Pine-Richland in Hersheypark Stadium.

Shawn Wilt blocked the potential game-tying extra point kick in the

second OT, allowing the Barons to escape with the victory. Pine-Richland had scored on a 1-yard run from Greg Hough moments earlier.

"I just saw an opening and went for it," said an exuberant Wilt afterward. "Jeremy Smith did a good job of taking out the guy in front of me and I just went after it. When it hit my hand, I couldn't believe it."

Wilt's block sent everybody on Central's sideline streaming onto the field for a wild celebration, while Pine-Richland's players slumped to the frozen turf in disbelief.

It was an amazing finish to a magnificent game that was played in the midst of a driving snowstorm in front of 5,202 frigid fans.

"This is probably the biggest thing that will happen to me in my life," Wilt exclaimed. "We put our blood, sweat and tears into this, and to win it all is unbelievable."

The victory is the 400th in school history for Manheim Central (15-0), which is the first Lancaster County school to win a state football championship. The Barons were making their first appearance in the state title game after falling eight times in the semifinals.

They snapped that semifinal jinx with last Saturday's 3-0 win over Strath Haven.

"This makes it all worthwhile," said Central coach Mike Williams. "We've lost games before where we didn't make plays, or we turned the ball over, or a coach's decision went awry. Something always kept us from winning.

"But this group of kids stayed on an even keel all year long. I think they definitely saved their best football for last."

They needed their best effort to subdue Pine-Richland, which played like a champion itself. Paced by a spectacular all-around effort by Hough, the Rams gave Central everything it could handle.

Hough, who was supposed to be lost for the season a few months ago when he suffered a torn tricep in his right arm, was making his second start since returning from the injury.

The 6-0, 205-pound senior was virtually unstoppable. He rushed for 126 yards and a touchdown on 34 carries, hauled in a 65-yard TD pass and returned a kickoff 91 yards for another score.

Pine-Richland (14-1) outgained Central 344-260 in total yards.

"They were hard to stop," said Williams. "Part of that is because they're a very good team, but part of it was we didn't tackle very well."

That might have had something to do with the weather conditions, which went from bad to awful over the course of the game.

Despite the best efforts of a group of volunteers, who rushed onto the field between plays to shovel off the yard lines, the field was covered by about an inch of snow by the time the game ended.

"I always thought it would be fun to play in the snow," said Central sophomore Jeremiha Hunter, who starts at running back and linebacker. "But it got frustrating after a while. It was freezing. You couldn't get a hold of anybody because your hands were so stiff. They just seemed to slip out of every tackle."

Hough's heroics weren't enough to stop Central, because several Barons came up big in the second half.

There was wideout Ryan Dennes, who got Central back in the game with a 73-yard punt return for a touchdown early in the third quarter. His 55-yard reception in the fourth quarter set up a go-ahead TD for the Barons.

There was quarterback Jarryd Moyer, who struggled early but threw a pair of second-half touchdown passes, including the game-winner in the second OT.

There was wideout Ryan Huber, who made his sixth reception of the season count. His 10-yard TD catch with 4:58 left in regulation on 4th-and-goal gave the Barons a short-lived 25-22 lead.

And there was Wilt, who hauled in a 10-yard TD strike from Moyer in the second OT, moments before he ended the game with his blocked kick.

He also made a huge defensive play late in regulation when he ripped a pass out of the hands of Pine-Richland wideout Neil Walker at the goal line on third down.

The Rams were forced to settle for a game-tying field goal that sent the game into overtime. If Walker had held onto the ball, the game would probably have ended right there.

"I might have been the guy who blocked the kick at the end, but I didn't win the game," said Wilt. "The team won this game. This is a win for Manheim Central, not just me."

Still, if Wilt hadn't blocked the kick, the Barons might still be playing. Neither team seemed able to stop the other in the second half — the lead changed hands eight times.

"I'm glad we ended the game when we did," quipped Williams. "I was running out of plays to call."

The Barons trailed 9-3 at halftime and were lucky to be that close. Pine-Richland attempted a 22-yard field goal on the final play of the second quarter but was thwarted when Central's Jeremy Smith blocked the kick.

"That was big," said Williams. "It gave us some momentum."

Dennes gave Central an even bigger boost early in the third quarter, when he fielded a punt at his own 27, raced to the outside and sprinted for a touchdown.

The score gave the Barons a 10-9 lead and appeared to put them in control. But Pine-Richland struck back on its next possession, as sophomore quarterback Jake Long hit Billy Massaro for a 65-yard touchdown. The Rams tried for a 2-point conversion but were turned away.

Central then regained the lead when Hunter (15 carries, 99 yards) capped a nine-play, 74-yard march with a 1-yard TD run. The drive was preserved by a crucial 15-yard penalty on Pine-Richland for roughing the kicker.

After a successful 2-point conversion, the Barons led 18-15 with 29 seconds left in the third quarter.

The lead didn't last long. Pine-Richland struck again when Hough took a flare pass from Long, eluded two Baron defenders and raced for a 65-yard score to give his team a 22-18 advantage with 11:39 left in regulation.

When Dennes was unable to return the ensuing kickoff past the 20, it appeared Central was in trouble.

But that's when Moyer came through. Facing a 3rd-and-long deep in his own territory, he hit Dennes in stride on a quick slant, and Dennes turned it into a 55-yard gain.

Central drove to the Pine-Richland 9, but the march appeared to falter when Moyer bobbled the snap on 3rd-and-goal.

The Barons went for it on fourth down, and Moyer (5-of-12, 68 yards) redeemed himself by eluding a fierce pass rush and hitting Huber in the middle of the end zone.

Again, it appeared Central was in control. But the Baron defense was unable to prevent the Rams from staging a 10-play, 55-yard march to set up Patrick Humes' game-tying 31-yard field goal with 1:01 left.

Pine-Richland got the ball first in overtime, and the Rams took a 32-25 lead when Walker scored on an end-around from the 8.

Central answered with a 1-yard plunge from Craig Gatchell. Moyer set up the short TD with a 9-yard scramble on first down.

The Barons got the ball first in the second OT, and Moyer wasted little time in giving his team the lead. He rolled to his right off a play-fake and hit Wilt, who scrambled through a Ram tackle and dove into the end zone.

The Rams made their last gasp when Hough scored from 1-yard out on 4th-and-goal, but Wilt's blocked kick finally ended it.

"We knew this was going to be a tough game," said Moyer afterward. "A lot of things went against us, but we played through it. We kept our heads up and kept battling."

Dec. 6:

AAAwesome!

Barons outduel Pine-Richland in double OT, winning on Wilt's blocked extra point, 39-38

By Ed Gruver
Intelligencer Journal

HERSHEY — Shawn Wilt, who staged an inspiring comeback from a near-season-ending leg fracture this season, provided the biggest play in Manheim Central football history Friday night.

And because he did, the Barons claimed their first-ever PIAA Class AAA championship.

With Hersheypark Stadium buffeted by gusting winds and blanketed by swirling snow, Wilt picked up key interference from teammates Jeremy Smith and Jeremiha Hunter, found a hole in Pine-Richland's offensive line and broke through to block kicker Patrick Humes' extra-point attempt in the game's second overtime.

Wilt's special teams heroics gave the Barons (15-0) a 39-38 double-OT win in a classic struggle that surpassed the high expectations surrounding the only state final this year to match two unbeaten teams. Moments before his game-deciding block, the Baron senior had provided another momentous play when he gathered in a 10-yard pass from QB Jarryd Moyer and beat left cornerback Brian Overton to the end zone.

"The Manheim Central Barons of 2003 won this game," said Wilt, putting an emphasis on Central's teamwork. "Jeremy Smith took the guy out like he was supposed to and Hunter stayed on the other side to pysche them out. (Pine-Richland) put a guy over there (to block Hunter), Smitty took his guy out and I had the hole and there it was.

"This was the most intense, biggest game. ... The win hasn't really set in yet. I'm tired and my head hurts, but I'm sure I'll feel great (today)."

Regarding his eventual game-winning TD catch, Wilt again pointed to Baron teamwork.

"Jarryd made a great throw," said Wilt, who fractured a fibula in his left leg Oct. 17 against Ephrata and was sidelined until the start of the district playoffs five weeks ago. "We wanted to win this game for Coach (Mike) Williams, and show everybody we could win."

The victory was the 400th in Central's history and 234th of Williams' career, and was marked by big plays on both sides and eight lead changes.

"The game was so back-and-forth it was unbelievable," Williams said. "To win the game the way we did is just a miracle.

"In my mind, we were doing well and then we weren't doing well, well and then not well. But in the end, the kids came through and it's typical of our style. We had it at the end.

"(Pine-Richland) is a great football team and it's a shame for them to lose. ... But here we are. First time here (in the final) and we're state champions. And nobody can take that away from us. Ever."

Central's championship did not come easy.

The Barons had to overcome not only the Western champion Rams (14-1), but wintry weather conditions that included a game-long mix of steady snow, icy, swirling winds, and freezing temperatures.

Central also had to play from behind for the first time this season. After the Barons took a 3-0 lead on Ryan Plowman's 27-yard field goal late in the first quarter, the Rams answered when senior Greg Hough fielded the ensuing kickoff at his 9-yard line, veered left, broke two tackles and tight-roped the Pine-Richland sideline en route to a 91-yard touchdown.

Humes' extra-point attempt sailed wide right in what turned out to be a crucial misplay. But he followed with a 35-yard field goal midway through the second quarter to give the Rams

a 9-3 lead at halftime. Jim Fawcett's block of a Jeremy Smith punt put Pine-Richland at Central's 16 with 1:04 to go in the half, but Smith responded by blocking Humes' 23-yard field goal attempt as time expired.

The second half offered a series of momentum-changing plays.

Central fired the first salvo when Ryan Dennes returned Hough's punt 73 yards for a score and a 10-9 Baron lead. Pine-Richland countered on its next series with a 55-yard scoring strike from QB Jake Long to tight end Billy Massaro.

The huge momentum swings stunned both sides.

"I thought we'd be out there slugging each other around," Rams coach Clair Altemus said. "But if you had asked me to predict this, I'd have said you're out of your mind. Especially with the snow and the way it was flying."

Said Moyer, "It seemed like we could be here forever, scoring back and forth."

Trailing 15-10, Central countered with a five-play, 54-yard scoring drive made possible by a costly roughing-the-punter penalty on the Rams. Sophomore back Jeremiha Hunter flowed through the middle on an inside trap for a 45-yard gain to the 1, then slammed into the end zone off the left side two plays later.

"It was a heckuva game the whole time," said Hunter, who ran for a team-high 99 yards on 15 carries.

"They score, we score. ... We kept going back and forth."

The Rams erased the 18-15 deficit on their next series. Hough, whose spinning runs and stiff straight-arms led to a game-high 126 yards on 34 carries, took Long's pass 65 yards for a score and a 25-22 lead with 11:39 to go in the game.

Central rallied back again, putting together a marathon 14-play, 83-yard drive keyed by Hunter's one-yard run on fourth-and-one, and Moyer's scrambling, TD pass to Ryan Huber on fourth-and-10.

Humes' 31-yard field goal with 1:01 left tied the game at 25 and forced overtime.

In the first OT, Rams' standout wide receiver/safety Neil Walker scored on an eight-yard run, but the Barons tied it on Craig Gatchell's one-yard dive up the middle.

Wilt's 10-yard TD catch gave Central a 39-32 lead. After Hough plowed

in behind massive right tackle Greg Conti, Wilt provided the final big play of the night, blocking Humes' extra-point attempt to set off Central's long-awaited celebration.

"This is the most exciting thing that's happened in my life," said Moyer. "It's great."

"This is absolutely incredible," senior two-way lineman Mike Byrne said. "We worked so hard in the off-season. ... We've been working since we were sophomores. We wanted it.

"Things happened the way they happened. End of story. We're state champs."

It was Williams, fittingly, who had the last word.

"This is the greatest victory in Manheim Central history, without a doubt," he said. "To win it on a blocked extra-point. ... If we didn't have that, who knows? We may still be playing."

True fans are willing to freeze, and go nuts, for their team.

Dec. 6:

GRAND CENTRAL!

Manheim goes wild as Barons storm to bone-chilling, heart-pounding state title

By Tom Murse and Susan Baldrige
Lancaster New Era

Just before midnight Friday, the snow-covered town of Manheim stirred to life.

Two fire engines — sirens blaring and lights flashing — escorted a pair of Manheim Central buses down Adele Avenue and into a parking lot overflowing with 500 cheering fans.

Car horns sounded.

Headlights flickered.

Camera bulbs flashed.

The storied Barons football team came home with its first state championship.

The town went nuts.

"We've lived here 20 years, and I'm happy — but it's almost relief, because we've been so close. We've been through this so many times before," said Brian Weidle, who heads the football team's booster club.

"To have it now, it's just like, wow!" he said. "This is a unique town. It's very supportive. They've waited a long time for this."

The Barons defeated the Pine-Richland Rams, 39-38, in a double-overtime thriller played in the middle of a snowstorm at Hersheypark Stadium.

"It was an emotional roller coaster — it was back and forth between two equal teams," said Jere Swarr, whose son Tyler is a wide receiver and defensive back.

"It was just unbelievable. I was freezing in the third period, but in the fourth quarter the cold just went away.

"It was that exciting," Swarr said.

The Barons won only after Shawn Wilt blocked a Rams point-after attempt that would have tied the game and sent the match into triple-overtime. It will go down as one of the greatest plays in Barons football history.

"It was almost like slow motion," said Mike Clair, the team's statistician, who was on the Barons sideline.

"People were jumping up and down and moving, but they really didn't know that they were jumping about for a while.

"It was hard for it to sink in," Clair said.

Barons fans knew immediately what happened.

"When that kick was blocked — pandemonium does not describe what was going on," said Kirk Radanovic, a Manheim Central school board member who was in the stands.

"It was the single most incredible sports feeling I've ever had," he said. "People went nuts. People just went crazy. People were just jumping.

"You were on the edge the entire game, the entire overtime," Radanovic said. "Every play could have been the last play. Then the final play was the last play, and we won — you can't describe that feeling, especially with the history, being in the hunt eight times before."

Freezing wind? Wet feet? Snowflakes like silver dollars?

Hey, Barons fans were too caught up in the game's ups and downs to care.

"It was like watching the game through a snow globe," said Carol Saylor, Manheim Central School District superintendent. "And actually during those two overtimes, I don't think anyone was cold. No one thought about it."

Only when the breathtaking game was over and Baron fans returned to their cars did they realize just how cold they really were, she said.

"Most everyone was dressed appropriately, although there were a few fans without shirts," said Saylor. "More power to them."

The Barons' undefeated season — and their big win Friday night — have certainly invigorated the town. Today, for example, Saylor's home phone was being answered: "State championship house."

Thousands of Manheim Central fans braved the treacherous, snow-covered roads to attend the game.

"There was no way, no way, we would miss the game," said Tom Zern, 48, a lifelong Manheim resident whose voice was raspy today.

"How many times do you go to a state championship and win a state championship?"

Zern, who took his wife Kim and daughter Carlyn to the game, marveled at the Barons and reminisced a bit.

"I thought back when I played for the Barons in the 1960s and 1970s, " he said. "We were co-champions for the league, but we weren't as good as they are now.

"Just seeing them play when it was so cold out there, the snow and wind conditions. I was thinking, 'How do they do it?' They played great."

The Barons' title is something the town will savor for a long, long time.

"It is a win for the community," said Swarr. "I don't think the kids will realize how lucky they are until they're older."

Dec. 6:

Title town

IN OUR VIEW

An Intelligencer Journal editorial

"Fame is the thirst of youth." So wrote Lord Byron nearly two centuries ago.

Friday night, the 2003 Manheim Central High School football team quenched that thirst with an exhilarating 39-38 overtime victory over a game Pine-Richland squad on a snow-covered field at HersheyPark Stadium.

It was a fitting performance for a championship game. Playing on the cusp of a Nor'easter, both teams traded blows and scores for nearly three hours in conditions that would close most major airports.

The game was seen by some as an affirmation of Manheim Central's football prowess. So often in the past, the Barons had reached the Class

AAA Eastern final only to fall short of competing in the state championship game. Their luck seemed to change last week when the Barons toppled nemesis Strath Haven, 3-0, to earn Eastern honors and guarantee them a spot opposite the Pine-Richland Rams.

After Central took a 3-0 lead, Pine-Richland offered a glimpse of what was to come when Greg Hough returned the ensuing kick-off 91 yards for a touchdown. The game see-sawed back and forth. Players on both teams gave extraordinary effort to keep the game close. A Pine-Richland field goal by Patrick Humes with 1:01 remaining in regulation forced overtime.

It was there that Manheim Central capitalized. The Barons answered a Pine-Richland score with one of their own, then took the lead on a touchdown pass to Shawn Wilt. Ryan Plowman's extra point gave the Barons a 39-32 lead. Hough answered with a touchdown to bring the Rams within one point but Wilt blocked the extra point try to bring the Barons their first state football title.

Both teams are worthy of being called state champions. In the end, the Barons came up with the key play that gave them the victory.

This game will live forever in Manheim history. The weather, the adversary and the adversity made for an extraordinary game. All that was missing was the signature voice of John Facenda, describing the action on the frozen tundra of HersheyPark Stadium.

Dec. 7:

JUST PERFECT

*In a snowy classic, Manheim Central finishes
its climb to top of Pennsylvania football*

By Mike Gross
Sunday News

HERSHEY — At one point, with athletes all around him jumping and diving and rising far above the biggest game of their lives, Sunday News photographer Jeff Ruppenthal's fingers gave out, literally too frozen to snap pictures. He simply couldn't push the button.

It was cold, people.

And it was as snowy as it was cold, and almost as windy as it was snowy, as Manheim Central and Pine-Richland made history at Hersheypark Stadium Friday night.

You had to be crazy to sit there for hours, just to watch a high-school football game.

Maybe, but 5,000-plus crazies witnessed Central 39, Pine-Richland 38 for the Class AAA state championship.

Another 5,000, at least, will someday claim they did.

2003 will be remembered as the year Central finally cashed its chips after so many near-misses, ratifying the greatness of its football program.

But it could be happily remembered just for this game, which reminded us that sport can seem magical. Somehow, the Barons and Rams were able to run and pass and catch and make a year's worth of big plays in conditions that might have postponed dog-sled races.

"I'm just amazed," Central coach Mike Williams said, speaking for everyone, "at the things high-school kids are able to do."

The one thing they weren't able to do, open-field tackle, only contributed to the drama. It seemed nearly impossible to do the usual plant-and-drive thing to bring down a ballcarrier.

That was the same for everybody, of course, and led to nine offensive plays of 40 yards or more, including a 91-yard kickoff return, a 72-yard punt return, and pass plays of 65 and 55 yards.

The kickoff return, by PR's Greg Hough, came early in the second quarter. The punt return, by Central's Ryan Dennes, came early in the third.

Then it was 10-9 Central, owing to a missed extra point.

It was only prelude, it turned out.

While Central quarterback Jarryd Moyer seemed to have the same trouble holding on to the ball anyone would, Pine-Richland QB Jake Long threw accurately throughout.

Long, a sophomore and only 5-foot-11, 180 pounds, threw for 177 yards, a surreal number on this night. He answered Dennes' TD with two strikes to speedy tight end Billy Massaro, the latter for a 55-yard touchdown.

Then the Rams stopped Central, but roughed the punter. Like the missed PAT, it haunted.

The Barons promptly got a 42-yard rumble up the middle from its superb soph, Jeremiha Hunter, leading to Hunter's TD plunge from one yard out.

But the Barons couldn't tackle Hough, who ran for 126 yards, not counting the kickoff return. And not counting a 65-yard, stiff-arming jaunt with a Long pass that gave PR a 22-18 lead.

Remember, all this is taking place in a frozen blizzard. And I can't drag my teen-ager away from PlayStation on the Fourth of July.

So now we're early in the fourth quarter, Central taking over and staring down the barrel of yet another postseason frustration. And promptly jumping offsides.

First-and-15, 88 yards away.

First down, nothing. Second down, nothing. But somewhere in here Moyer was gaining a grasp of the ball and the occasion. On third-and-16 he drilled Eric Meyers for 42 yards into Pine-Richland territory.

The Barons started chugging now, mostly straight ahead, mostly behind the precocious Hunter, who ran for 99 yards.

They appeared to stall at the 7, and then Moyer fumbled a center exchange, recovering it back at the 10.

Fourth-and-goal, five minutes left, Central down four. Was it the wind howling or the ghosts?

And Moyer came up huge. He scrambled, rolled, looked, looked and finally found Ryan Huber in the end zone, just his sixth catch of the year. 25-22.

What's wild, looking back, is how far it was from being over.

With regulation time waning, Pine-Richland drove back behind its studs, Hough and wideout Neil Walker.

Long hit Walker for 32 yards to the Central 41. Then Hough ran four straight times, to the 14. But here Central rose up, Shawn Wilt brilliantly breaking up a pass to Walker in the end zone. Wilt, we'll learn, was just getting warmed up, so to speak.

The Rams' kicker, Patrick Humes, who had missed that extra point and had a field goal blocked, drilled a 31-yarder into the swirling flakes to tie it.

Strange and amazing, how far the offenses were ahead of the defenses as they headed into overtime. It seemed they might play until the weather broke.

Stranger, Williams had a kept a weapon shielded until now: Moyer rolling to his right and making a play.

"We were kind of saving that for the right time," he said. Think overtime in a state final qualifies?

The Rams scored first, on Walker's 7-yard run. Central matched, Moyer rolling and keeping for 10 yards to the 1, Craig Gatchell taking it from there.

In the second OT Central went first, scoring when Moyer rolled again and found Wilt. Pine-Richland answered on four straight Hough runs, as newspaper deadlines dissolved in the cold.

Except that there was this business of the extra point. Williams' film study had revealed PR might be vulnerable to kick-blocks, and indeed the Barons had blocked a field goal just before halftime.

Now Central overloaded the left side of the Rams' line, forcing one lineman to choose between blocking Wilt or someone else. He chose someone else.

Wilt flew to the ball, and made the play that will make him a hero in his hometown for life.

The next few moments were unforgettable, delicious ecstasy and bitter agony side by side.

Pine-Richland's Greg Conti, an absolutely monstrous two-way lineman, might have been the best player on the field. Now he grabbed one of his coaches like a traumatized child seeking his father and held on, motionless, endlessly.

Thirty feet away, giddy Barons flopped on their backs and made snow angels.

Then Williams was on the shoulders of his players, cradling the trophy in one arm, raising the other high in triumph.

That looked exactly right. Could've been a statue.

No doubt this was all very compelling on TV. But somehow high-school sports never quite translate on the tube, at least for me. Especially in this case. You really had to be there.

So was it crazy to watch, or crazy not to?

That's your call. It can't be made from a heated press box.

I can tell you this: It was the best football game I've ever seen.

SECTION II RECORD: 7-0   2003   OVERALL RECORD: 15-0

ROW ONE: Tyler McCauley, Jared Gibble, Rob Trovato, Neil Hershey, Mike Byrne, Jarryd Moyer, Kevin Hershey, Ryan Buchter, Steve Petrosky. ROW TWO: Eric Meyers, Kevin Krause, Ryan Dennes, Shawn Wilt, Ben Engle, Jeremy Smith, Grant Kline, Miles Groff. ROW THREE: Glenn Han son, Adam Manz, Ty Leese, Kevin Yeagle, Billy Raffensperger, Tyler Reifsnyder, Tom Kirby, Ryan Huber, Tyler Swarr. ROW FOUR: Blake Aston, Brandon Miller, Zach Buchmoyer, Graham Zug, Craig Gatchell, Steve Weidle, Jeremiha Hunter, Jason Morgan, Brett Shireman. ROW FIVE: Nate Mast, Andy Wilson, Shawn Ream, Andy Trafford, Zach Hower, Jeremy Greenly, Garrett Anderson, Jay Campbell, Grant Clift. ROW SIX: Andy Kirchner, Jon Simmavath, Eli Esh, Brad Werley, Ben Delp, Kyle Peterson, Tim Meyers, Jeff Ochoa. ROW SEVEN: George May, Chuck Wenger, Joey Brubaker, Carl Minieri, Jarred Rineer, Eric Rhoads, Dan Trafford, Seth Weidle, Bruce Kilmoyer, Mitch Heinsey. ROW EIGHT: Joe Mack, Barry Lewis, John Brubaker, Mike Williams, Dave Hahn, Brian Hunter, Chad Enck, Rick Smith. MISSING: Ryan Plowman, John Phillips, Gary Weaver, Pat Weaver, George Derbyshire.

Photo credits:

Pages 5, 10, 25, 32, 47, 49, 57 (top), 65 (top), 69 (top and bottom right), 115 (both), 127 and 134 by **Jeff Ruppenthal**; pages 38, 40 (both), 42 (bottom), 59, 61, 70 and 130 by **Dan Marschka**; pages 9, 24, 27, 28, 35, 37, 55, 56, 57 (bottom), 65 (bottom), 69 (bottom left), 107 and 142 by **Tom Amico**; pages 20, 23, 46, 48, 62, 94, 117, 118 by **Andrew Blackburn**; pages 21, 43, 66, 67 (all), 68, 101 by **Barry Zecher**; pages 11, 14, 15, 26, 51 by **Vinny Tennis**; pages 30 (both), 42 (top), 80 by **Suzette Wenger**; page 17 by **Blaine Shahan**; page 84 by **Deb Grove**.

Acknowledgements

I would like to recognize and thank the many, many people and institutions who contributed to this project. Among them:

Mike Williams, whose impact included, but was not limited to, one long sit-down interview and several shorter ones, and who might be the most media-wise coach in the history of high-school football.

The players and coaches of the 2003 team who sat for interviews. I won't list all their names because, if you've read the book, you already know them. I'm glad I know them. Couldn't have done it without you, fellas. Remarkably, every single one of you provided something no one else did.

Manheim Central athletic director George Derbyshire, Pine-Richland coach Clair Altemus, player Greg Conti and Robert Lombardi of the PIAA also provided useful and compelling interviews and information.

Brian Hunter, who met me for lunch at a York diner and, in lavish detail, told his side of a complicated and critical part of the story.

The Manheim Touchdown Club, whose members have produced two books — "The History of Manheim Central Football 1947-2012,' and the 2003 football banquet program — that were constant and invaluable references.

During the 2003 season, Ed Gruver, Kevin Freeman and Jeff Reinhart covered the Barons, about as well as it can be done, for Lancaster Newspapers. Some of their work appears here, and all of it informs everything here.

The same goes for the other LNP writers who wrote about the '03 Barons: Susan Baldridge, Mike Byrne's uncle Dave, Carla Di Fonzo, the late Dennis Fisher, Jason Guarente, Tom Murse, Justin Quinn, P.J. Reilly, Ryan Robinson,

Jon Rutter, Joel Schreiner, Keith Schweigert, Andrew Sheely, Eric Stark and the late Harold Zeigler.

The superb photos in the book were produced, largely in dog-sled-race conditions, by Jeff Ruppenthal, Dan Marschka, Suzette Wenger, Marty Heisey, Blaine Shahan, Andrew Blackburn, Vinny Tennis, Barry Zecker, Tom Amico and Deb Grove. Marschka assumed the awful burden of taking the author's photo on the back cover.

Also in the LNP newsroom, Michael Long, a giant among wordsmiths, copy-edited the heck out of the text. Ruppenthal acted as photo editor. Roxanne McRoberts paginated the book, and Chris Emlet designed the cover. These four people, in particular, went above and beyond in committing their time and talent to someone else's idea. I am grateful.

Other useful copy-editing came from Ernie Schreiber, Paula Wolf, and Barbara Hough Roda. LNP sports editor Laura Thompson and everyone else in the paper's sports department, to put it bluntly, covered my butt while I slogged through this thing.

My old sportswriting buddy Gordie Jones provided advice, copy-editing and, as always, laughs. Other ink-stained pals, Frank "The Sportswriting Gourmet" Bodani of the York Daily Record and David Jones of the Harrisburg Patriot-News, produced information and clarity.

This book was my idea, but it wouldn't exist without the enthusiastic support of Robert M. Krasne, publisher and president of Lancaster Newspaper Inc., Executive Editor Ernie Schreiber and Robert Mason, president of Intelligencer Printing Company. Linda Anspach of Intelligencer Printing Company shepherded the project in numerous ways.

My wife, Debra, and sons, Ben and Adam, continue to put up with my struggle to get out of my own way. My in-laws, Jim and Ethel Murray, let me have their cabin for a couple of days of electronic-distraction-free writing. Again, bigger deals than they sound.

Finally, I'd like to salute, for reasons too varied to outline here, Jim Hersh and Steve Snyder, John Updike and David Foster Wallace, Bill James and Dan Jenkins, everyone at A&M Pizza (in Lebanon and Manheim) and Shire Pharmaceuticals, makers of Adderall, without which I'd probably still be on about Chapter Three right now, and because of which I am ineligible to play major league baseball.

To all of you, and anyone I forgot, thanks.

Mike Gross
September, 2013